Angel Quest

A Journey Into Wisdom

An Adventure Story
By Thomas Charles Sannar

About the Author

Tom Sannar has been a teacher, a California trial attorney and a minister. He is currently serving as the Co-Pastor of New Thought Community Church in Milwaukee, Wisconsin with his wife Gisela. Married for thirty years, Tom and Gisela have two children, Torsten who is an actor in Los Angeles and Elise who is employed by Teach for America and is teaching in the inner city schools in Los Angeles. Tom and Gisela reside in Milwaukee.

11/98

Angel Wisdom Publishing
1029 N. Jackson, Suite 1401A
Milwaukee, Wisconsin 53202

First Printing, August 1996
Library of Congress Catalog Card Number:
ISBN 0-9653807-77

Printed in the United States of America

Bookstore

Dedication

I dedicate this book to my wife, Gisela, without whom this adventure could never have been written and published. During all those times when I lost my center and seemed to have forgotten my Source, she has always been there to love and forgive me.

When I began writing Angel Quest, I was living in Fresno, California. As I finished the last chapter, I continued to pray that I would be led to the perfect people who would help me disseminate this important knowledge to the public. I remember the words that came to me at the end of the book:

"Write," the voices said. "We will help you remember. Write the truth about angels. Don't concern yourself with the outcome. Just write. The ways and means will be provided for your information to become public. You are fulfilling your mission."

As I began to write, I knew everything was unfolding perfectly. I embraced my mission. I felt the energy, the passion, the power, the love of my whole life.

"I am completing the first part of the plan," I thought. "The time is arriving. All I need to do is get out of the way and let it happen. And it is."

As I write this dedication, I find myself living in Milwaukee, Wisconsin. I believe the angels brought me here to find the perfect artist and illustrator in the person of Joyce Gust. How could I have known that she understood intuitively and was already expressing in her paintings what I was attempting to convey.

And at the Knickerbocker Cafe in downtown Milwaukee, Lee Ann Fagan Dzelzkalns appeared in my life, the perfect advisor and inspirational friend. These things do not happen by accident.

Throughout my incredible journey with the angels over the last two years, during my inspirations and my desperations, the unconditional love, compassion and forgiveness of my wife, Gisela has sustained me.

To my wife, Gisela, who demonstrates on a daily basis, the unconditional love of the angels, I dedicate this book.

Angel Wisdom Publishing is a branch of Angel Wisdom™

The vision of Angel Wisdom™ is to awaken humanity through Wisdom. We are here to:

Open Minds
through the clear teaching of Wisdom.

Heal Hearts
through the integrating power of Love.

Nurture Souls
through facilitating angel groups in Action.

The Seven Truths Of The Angels

1. ## We live in a spiritual universe.
   There are many dimensions in the universe. We do not live in a physical universe. We live in a spiritual universe.

2. ## Evil is the result of human ignorance.
   The devil or demons will never come into the mind of a person who focuses on God, goodness and love.

3. ## We are spiritual energy systems.
   All people have seven energy systems within their 'psycho-noetic body' that correspond to the seven Archangels.

4. ## We are to ask with open hearts.
   When we ask with an open heart to know the truth about angels, our request will be granted.

5. ## We are to embrace all aspects of life.
   When we learn to embrace, all aspects of life, (what we call good and bad, including death) with wonder and compassion, we begin to understand the true meaning of love.

6. ## We are here to heal our planet through love.
   It is the purpose for human beings to bring peace to planet Earth, through the healing power of love.

7. ## We are to take a leap of faith.
   We are to step forward, move into the light that we cannot see, but the light our soul knows.

Acknowledgments

I am so grateful for all the loving friends who supported me and knew with me the truth and power of this book, especially our wonderful church congregations in Fresno and Milwaukee.

To Gisela, who would listen patiently to the story as it unfolded, supporting me all the way.

To my children, Torsten and Elise, who consistently demonstrate the wisdom of angels in their lives.

To Shari Hemingway, who spent hours and hours, transcribing and editing the first drafts of the manuscript.

To Connie Lindholm, who led me to a great artist of the angels.

To Joyce Gust, who revealed the essence of the angels in her paintings and to her wonderful and supportive husband, Mel.

To Lee Ann, who came into my life at the perfect right moment, to guide me to publish Angel Quest and who is fulfilling her destiny as a great teacher of Truth.

To Heritage Graphics of Milwaukee, and their talented graphic artist, Dave Dumke, who was instrumental in the book design.

To Bookcrafters, of Chelsea, Michigan, whose professional expertise printed a first quality book.

And finally to Cleo, the wise old one and the innocent child who provided the inspiration and the wisdom for Angel Quest.

Table of Contents

Foreword

Even before this manuscript was published, questions were asked about how it came into being. Is it fiction or is it based on fact? Like *The Celestine Prophecy, Angel Quest* is an adventure story.

The characters in the story are fictional. The facts are that, sometime between Christmas and New Year's 1993, I heard a voice deep within tell me to be open about angels. Subsequent events began to almost conspire so that I was supplied with a great deal of information about angels.

Around the middle of January 1994, I awakened from a deep sleep at 3 a.m. and was told to get up and start writing. For about four months, on and off, a voice would call to me in my sleep, wake me in the early morning hours, and tell me to write. The voice never identified itself as an angel and never told me what to write. The writing is not automatic or "channeled," but I do believe it is inspired. The inner voice just told me to be open and receptive and information would be revealed to me.

There is much information written in this book about which I had no prior knowledge. In fact, I marvel at many of these revealed ideas each time I reread it.

So, was this book written with the assistance of angelic beings? Are angels only symbols of higher power and inspiration in each of us? Is this adventure story indeed the truth about angels? Readers will have to make that decision for themselves. As for me, I am still open. More information is forthcoming every day.

I believe that Angel Quest is a dynamic, progressive and growing process of truth. This truth is given to us exactly when we need to know it. I also believe there are others who know the same truth. By proclaiming what we know openly, at this stage of human development, we help awaken the planet and prepare it for its coming transformation.

And so, I invite you into an experiment of openness and to the possibility that the presence of angels is real. We believe that human beings are immortal souls in disguise and take on physical form.

Consider the possibility that there are other kinds of beings who represent God, and who assist humans from dimensions that are not physical and who are willing, if we are open, to make their presence known.

May *Angel Quest: A Journey Into Wisdom* awaken and alert you to your angels and aid you in your own personal quest for truth in your life.

Introduction

"It's time to take the walk, the journey towards the discovery, the discovery of yourself, the discovery of your purpose, the discovery of your relationship with the Earth. But, there is one thing I must tell you. If you begin this walk, you cannot turn back until you've completed the journey. You will become a different person. Your life will change, and, in many ways, you will be thrown out of your old comfort zones. You will feel a much greater responsibility and love for others. You will become less self-involved. Things will become more ambiguous. What used to be black and white answers will no longer be so. You will learn the capacity to see and feel from the position of many different people at the same time. You will feel their pain, their anxiety, their fears. We will teach you how to do this. We will teach you how to merge with the consciousness of other sentient beings so that you can know the diversity and complexities of life. For amidst the joys and sorrows of people, you will also know the truth and be able to help guide them towards the truth."

When I heard these words echo in my soul, I knew there could be no turning back. Once I made the decision, the Universe would conspire to come to my aid.

By making the decision to read this book, you may be inspired to continue the journey. If it is your heart's desire, the ways and means for the fulfillment of your journey will be provided for you. To continue will take discipline, dedication and relentless desire, but if you choose to help, you will also become a messenger to help bring about the coming transformation and to help alleviate fear and suffering on the planet.

You have a guardian angel. You may not call it that. You may call it "the still small voice" within you. But if you open your heart and ask, the voice will come to you, to guard you, to guide you on your journey to the truth of your being.

That's how this book came about. It started with the question, Why do so many people believe in angels? As soon as I asked that question, a voice inside me told me to be open, to pray, and to start doing research on the nature of angels. And so I started.

Within two days of my first question, I had my first experience with angels. I didn't see an angel, but I felt its presence so strongly that I knew I had been visited. I felt its warmth, and I felt its love. You don't have to see angels to know they are there.

My journey has begun and it will not end until the purpose for which I came has been fulfilled. The story of my angel quest will open your heart to the wisdom of the angels, a wisdom so profound that you may wish to join me and become a true messenger, a messenger of the angels, an angel to the angels.

Chapter One

Be Open About Angels

"If you are open, the angels will assist you and make their presence known, for you have already entertained angels unaware."

How much time had gone by? Where was I? I remembered the fog, the lights of the truck, hitting my brakes and swerving. I looked around. I saw a field below me. Oh my God, I thought. There is a body down there. He needs help. I need to call the highway patrol. How can I help him?

Wait a minute. How can I be seeing what I'm seeing? Where am I? I'm up in the air. What am I holding on to? I'm floating in the air. I'm floating over this field!

In the distance, I could see my car, the road, and the fog. It didn't seem to be as thick now. My attention then went back to the form, the body. I recognized that body. I had seen it before. It seemed so helpless, so lifeless, in a way, so repugnant. I almost didn't want to recognize it as me. How could it be me, when I'm here? But as that thought passed through my mind, I suddenly turned and started to move upward through the fog, above the fog, to the darkness of the night, and into the starry sky.

Up, up, I went, faster and faster. And as I watched, I saw a light approaching. Was I moving towards it, or was it moving towards me? Within seconds, I was in the light. It was like a tunnel. At first, the tunnel was opaque and dim. Up ahead I could see it brighter and brighter. I was traveling very fast through this tunnel.

I could hear sounds, the mingling of different sounds somehow creating a harmonious hum. I had heard that humming before somewhere in my past, but I couldn't remember where. It was like a vibration penetrating through me. I had read about people who had near-death experiences, who had been bathed in light. But I was immersed in the most beautiful and indescribable sound. I could actually feel it. The sound was rushing towards me and through me like the wind. But there was no resistance. It was like little particles of sound dancing around me, dancing in a pulsating rhythm, moving continuously through me.

Then there was the light. I could feel its presence. It was all around me. As far as I could look, there was light. The sound and the light came together, and I couldn't tell one from the other. Was I seeing it, hearing it, or feeling it? All three. But, mostly, I was feeling it. I could feel the presence of the wonderful golden light immersed in a heavenly sound. I could feel its warmth, but not warmth in the form of heat, but in the form of extreme coziness. All during this time, I continued to move with great speed. It felt like being in a current, a current of light and sound and voices. One part of the current was moving with me, one part was moving away from me, to where it had come from.

How long I continued, I do not know. Soon, I felt myself slowing down in this light. Then I just seemed to hover in one place. I felt a tremendous presence in the light and a feeling of indescribable love. It was as if this light-sound-energy was caressing me, just giving of itself, giving its energy to me.

In my early spiritual experiences back on Earth, I had felt something like this, a love, a power, like a gravitational force, moving into my body and caressing every cell. This experience was even more overwhelming. I knew that I was loved with an everlasting love. Something very profound within me began to stir. I was both entranced and entrained in its very presence. I was breathing in this love, feeling it in every aspect of my being. And I felt the presence blending and dancing within me.

I could not call it my body, for I did not know if I was in a body. It simply felt like dancing light merging with dancing light. I was so much into the experience that I lost all sense of time, space and orientation.

Then it seemed as if the light spoke, not in words, but in thoughts and in feelings. It said, "Don't be afraid. There's nothing to fear ever. I am here to help you, to guide you, to nurture you. I have always been with you, and I will never desert you."

I felt a humming inside of me, an urge to start singing. The light and the sound joined together as one, and I could feel its vibration, and I really knew that it was telling me the truth. It had always been with me, and would always be with me.

I only write now, upon reflection, in an attempt to put this experience into human words so that others might understand. It was an experience beyond experience. It was a mingling and a merging that felt like my heart had opened up, like my heart was breaking, expanding until the sound, the light, and I merged as one. There was no difference. I was the light. I was the love. I was the sound. I was the feeling of it all. Just remembering it, I am able to feel the experience as if it is happening all over again.

How did it all begin? It started with a simple request . I simply wanted to know the truth about angels. And I thought I'd find the answer in a library! Little did I know. I remember that statement, "Be careful what you ask for, 'cause you're likely to get it." Boy, did I get it. So, maybe I'd better start at the beginning and explain just how these events transpired.

It was about 2 a.m. on an early Tuesday morning, sometime between Christmas and New Year's. I've always been a night person, and I have developed this weird habit of journal writing and introspection during the late evening and early morning hours. I was thinking about the coming year and what I wanted to accomplish. For the past three years, I had been in an active prayer meditation group. I was taught that there is a Divine Intelligence in the universe and this Intelligence is "on purpose." I was also taught to ask God to reveal to me what I needed to know about the coming year and to guide me and direct me in my life.

And so as I sat in meditation, listening for an answer, all of a sudden, one word came to me loud and clear. Angels.

Angels? What about angels? I didn't know anything about angels and had rarely given them a thought. But I wrote the word angels in my journal and then moved my mind to other areas of the new year. For the seventh year in a row I wrote: I will lose thirty pounds this year. I am slim, trim and healthy. Feeling better, I sliced myself two large pieces of mozzarella cheese, poured myself a cup of hot chocolate made with Nutra-sweet, and went to bed.

The next morning when I arrived at my office, I noticed that someone had placed a copy of Time magazine on my desk. The cover showed pictures of angels. The leading article inside wondered why so many people were obsessed with the topic. I learned a long time ago that when a word or idea comes to you, and then something happens that puts the same idea in your face from another source, you're supposed to pay attention.

Okay. So I was supposed to pay attention to angels this year. I read the article and it said that sixty-nine per cent of the American public believe in angels. Forty-six per cent believe they have their own guardian angels watching over them. Thirty-two per cent of them said they had personal contact with angels. I was amazed. Who were these angels anyway? Where did they come from? What did they look like? Were they all the same? Did they all have wings? I began to get my investigative newspaper consciousness in gear. I decided that I was going to find out about angels.

So I started to ask a few friends what they knew. Before I knew it, I was given a few books, including *Paradise Lost* by Milton. I meditated again the following night and asked, What am I supposed to know about angels? Why am I supposed to know it? The words that came to me were simply this, "Be open about angels." And so my adventure began.

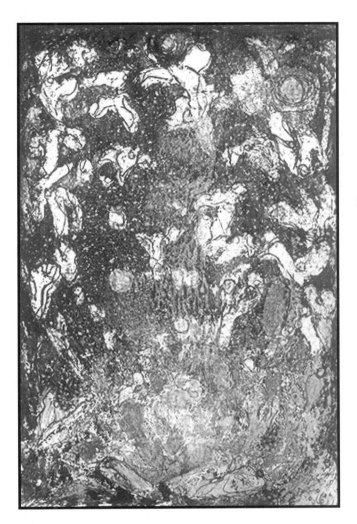

Chapter Two

Lost and Found Again

"Allow the tears to flow, let the pain of your life to come to the surface, where it can be immersed in the healing power of love. Allow yourself to feel very open and very vulnerable and you will come to the realization that God really is love. And you will be glad to be alive."

I remember when I was a little boy, about three years old, I knew I could fly. I was never afraid of high places because something inside of me knew that if I fell, I would softly float to the ground. But after I fell off a roof, dove into a sand box and ended up with a few stitches, I decided to reevaluate my position. There was something about this world I was in that seemed very different and unfamiliar to me.

From an early age, I also knew that my parents, my sister and my brother were not really related to me. I always felt alone. When I was five years old, my family were still strangers to me. But, fortunately, I discovered little girls, who were infinitely nicer than the little boys and a lot more fun. And to this day, I have never changed my mind about that.

My parents took me to church, they dressed me up in short pants, and we sang all the hymns. But the only thing I learned was that there was a great deal of confusion about Christianity, Jesus, God and the Holy Spirit. It was very unclear to me whether Jesus was a man, a God-Man, or was God pretending to be Jesus? Or was he some kind of fictitious person that people told stories about, like Santa Claus? But I quickly learned that in order to be accepted I had to show that I agreed with what everyone else thought. As soon as I could figure out what everyone else thought, then I would think the same thing.

As might be expected, I had a rough time conforming to the beliefs of any groups, especially the religious ones. I discovered that there were hundreds of religious groups which claimed that they knew the absolute truth about God and Jesus. They said that their way was the only way. I was very puzzled. I knew that there had to be more than one way to understand God. Were these people all so scared that they just became rigid?

By the time I was twelve, I figured that God was made up and Jesus probably was, too. And, besides, nothing that I heard was relevant to my life. I met my first love and had a deep desire to merge with her. I don't want to give the wrong impression. I was only twelve, so I don't mean physically merge. Although I knew what sex was intellectually, I had no confidence when it came to experimenting. I found out much later that my 'desire to merge' was really on a soul level, that most likely, she and I had known each other in another dimension. But, unfortunately, she left my life when I was thirteen, because her mother was afraid that we were too serious. This was too bad, because, even today, I know that we would have been best friends. Knowing what I know now, I really believe I'll see her again.

After that experience with first love, I was very lonely. It was hard to make more than superficial friends. But when I was about sixteen, I started to have what some people might call 'spiritual experiences'. It was like I was remembering things from before I was born.

I had a real vivid dream. In the dream, the people of the Earth were at the brink of war. Negotiations between the United States and Russia had completely broken down. There was silence from both governments. People were really scared. They stayed home from work and just waited. Everyone knew at the gut level that somehow humanity had gone too far. We had crossed the line of no return. Nuclear war and the destruction of the planet seemed inevitable. And then something very strange happened.

Next door to my house was a big field. About 4 p.m. in the afternoon, something that could only be described as a flying saucer landed on the field. Everyone in the neighborhood ran out of their houses and stood around the edge of the field, keeping their distance from the spacecraft. As we watched intently, the top of the saucer began to open. There appeared a huge eye that looked like a mechanical beacon. The eye came out from an opening at the top like a periscope from a submarine. No one could move. No one could run away. We were all transfixed. This huge eye began to rotate, and as it did, it sent out a beam. As the beam moved in a circular fashion, it hit each person. I saw people just fall down, faint dead away. I could not run. I could not scream. I simply watched in fascination as the beam swept around. I knew it would hit everyone, including me. No one would escape. I waited and watched, almost with a sense of resignation. When the beam was finally aimed at me, I looked directly into the huge, intelligent eye. Then, everything went completely black.

In the dream, I woke up and I was in my own bed. I ran downstairs. My parents were there, the house was there, the neighborhood was there, and everything was fine. The Earth was just like before. But, the threat of war was over.

We all knew that somehow we had been saved. No one talked about the flying saucer. There was no trace of its existence. Governments functioned just like before. We went about the business of living our lives just like before, except we knew deep down, at some unconscious level, that somehow a force of much greater intelligence had intervened on our planet. What happened in my neighborhood had happened all over the world. We knew we were saved and there would be no more war. Although we had free will and could do pretty much what we wanted to down here on the Earth, there was some unseen force that was providing us with ultimate protection. We would never be permitted to destroy ourselves. This force would see to that.

Even in my personal life, I kept recalling the times that I could have died, only to be miraculously saved. One time I was spinning across four lanes of highway at oncoming traffic. Another time, I was speeding down a winding mountain road at high speed, trying to drive the car, kiss my girlfriend and drink wine, all at the same time. Still another time, I remember driving up a Bay Bridge off-ramp the wrong way, seeing the oncoming traffic, their headlights moving towards my vehicle. Somehow, I always averted disaster. At the time, I attributed it to luck. But now I know that there was someone watching over me. I have learned that I am really not supposed to leave this planet until I've completed my mission.

I started to have experiences of unity and oneness. I began to know at a very deep level that all life was interconnected. Right before my seventeenth birthday, I had an experience where I absolutely knew the truth about the Earth, the universe, and why we are here. The greatest feeling of joy swept over me, and it was like one ultimate truth revealed in a glorious instant. I began to laugh and knew that if only I could keep this feeling, I would solve all the riddles of the universe. Unfortunately, I began to start analyzing and characterizing my feelings and the experience disappeared.

I so much wanted to have that same feeling again. And so I began a spiritual search for the 'true religion'. I was twenty years old when I concluded that I could find God only in a Buddhist monastery. I remember one day sitting on a hill, it was around the first week of June, when the notion came to me that if I really wanted to experience God, I would have to give up all of the pleasures of the world and subject myself to the rigors of the monastery. I made a conscious decision that day. I decided to suppress my desire for God and rechannel it in finding love in another person. I remembered that I had found it when I was thirteen, and I knew that I could find it again.

I would find the perfect person who would be my soul mate, who would love me with an everlasting love. We would merge together in the essence of Divine Love. But the more I looked, the more frustrated I became. Just when I thought I had found her, something would happen, and the relationship would deteriorate and I would be alone again. Occasionally I would be awakened by an inner voice, but these experiences became fewer and farther between. One time, I walked into a Christian Science Church. I was greeted with a very simple phrase on the wall, 'God Is Love'. I remember my soul knowing this to be the truth, but the memory faded, and I was again alone.

In college I decided to major in journalism and I set my sights on landing a job with a big city newspaper. During these years, I became more and more jaded about religion. I learned to smoke, drink and become socially acceptable. When I graduated from college in 1972, I was fortunate enough to land a newspaper job with a small paper in a farming town in Northern California. Over the years, I moved from one small paper to another, always making a living, but not much of a life.

In 1980, when I was working in San Luis Obispo, covering city hall and reviewing movies, I met a woman who was to become my wife. She loved me, but I never could understand why. I felt she was smothering me. In retrospect, I know she was simply opening her heart to me. Most of the time I felt trapped. We were married for nine years. I know now that she was trying to teach me the true meaning of love, but at that time I wasn't much interested. I was already set in my ways. I pretty much thought life was pointless. There was way too much suffering in the world, and I couldn't see any end to it. Most of the religious people I knew were phonies, or at least I thought they were phonies. I had enough sense to know materialism was a dead-end street. I had this kind of constant dull ache surrounding my whole body.

The only time the ache went away was when I got drunk, which was quite often. I didn't drink during work or in the day time, so I didn't have a problem keeping my job. In fact, drinking was sort of the common thread between me and my editor. He was in his early sixties, was generally down on life, and could expound ad nauseam on how crummy the world was. We spent many a night together at a local bar around the corner from the paper, while my wife waited at home to see if I would ever snap out of it. Finally, she got tired of waiting and divorced me. Fortunately, we didn't have any kids, so I just kind of stumbled and drank through the divorce proceedings, pretending that it really didn't bother me. And so, in addition to drinking and smoking more, being separated and lonely again, I began to look puffy and pudgy.

I remember about three weeks after my wife left me, I woke up around 10 a.m. on a Sunday morning. I looked in the mirror at a real hung over face and commented to myself, 'I really don't care for your company anymore.' I felt I had really hit bottom.

Now I wish I could say I had some kind of revelation. I didn't. I got fired from my job. The paper was losing money, but because I had been there six years, they gave me six months to try to locate another job. After four months of looking, I finally found another newspaper job as a religious editor, a couple hundred miles away in the San Joaquin Valley. When I was hired, they told me that it was my job to get along with the various ministerial associations, the Catholic Church, and the Jewish Rabbi. They also told me, I guess my former editor said something to them, that if I was ever caught drinking, I would lose my job.

Well, a funny thing happened. Maybe it was mid-life crisis in reverse, but I really started to like my job, and I really started to feel more at home. As I met more ministers and priests and the city's two rabbis, I became interested in their lives, both as human beings and spiritual leaders. To my surprise, although I found some of them very dogmatic, I also found them to be sincere seekers of spiritual truth. Each in his own way was trying to bring the Love of God to the community.

I stopped drinking and smoking completely, except for an occasional beer. I joined a gym. With the exception of that little "pot beer belly," I actually was proud of my body. I found myself liking my job more and more and even began to like myself a little. I located a small church that emphasized meditation and prayer and joined a prayer group that met once a week. It was here that I learned to meditate. One night God really opened my heart and I felt the love of Holy Spirit expand in my chest. I was immersed in a feeling of love that was indescribable. It is difficult to write about, both because I am not articulate enough and also because the feeling cannot be described. The tears just began to flow. All of the pain in my life came to the surface that night, and then I knew that the experiences I had had when I was younger were real. They came back to me, breaking through the shell of my defenses. For the first time, I felt very open and very vulnerable. I remember repeating over and over to myself, "God really is love. God really is love." And I was glad to be alive.

Chapter Three
The Woman from North Fork

"I am Cleo, revealing to you the wisdom and beauty of your soul."

ANGEL QUEST

In early January I received a phone call from a friend of mine named Phoebe.

"Hey, I hear through the grapevine you're interested in learning more about angels," she said.

"Yeah. That's right," I said.

"Well, there's this woman who lives in North Fork who is an angelologist," she informed me.

"A what?" I asked.

"An angelologist," she said. "You know, like an anthropologist or an archeologist, only it's someone who digs into angels. Anyway, she knows a lot about angels. She's real old, and she lives by herself out in the country. People say she's a little strange and a bit eccentric, but she really knows her angels. You should go see her."

"Yeah. Sounds interesting. Maybe I will," I said, actually feeling a little reluctant.

Phoebe and I talked for a while longer about this odd woman and about angels. It turned out that Phoebe didn't really know too much about this woman, but she did know that her name was Cleo and that she lived in the foothills, not too far from Fresno.

Early the next morning, I debated whether or not to call the old woman. She sounded really odd and the last thing I needed was to get involved with a crazy person. But I had a gut feeling that I really needed to call her, that I was supposed to call her. So thinking, "Oh, well. What have I got to lose?", I looked her number up in the book and gave her a call.

Our conversation was very brief. I introduced myself, explained that I got her name from a friend, that I was currently doing research on angels and asked if she would be willing to see me. She said with a very kind and grandmotherly voice that she would be happy to see me if I could drive up that very morning because that was the only time she had available. I said that I could and that I would be there around 10 a.m.

It takes about an hour from my house to drive to the little town of North Fork. It was a foggy morning. This time of the year, fog covers the San Joaquin Valley. It usually burns off by early afternoon and returns again by nightfall. It was one of those depressing kind of days. The fog had lifted to about three hundred feet above the valley floor. It was impossible to see the sunshine. But if you drive up into the foothills, about a thousand feet high, the fog breaks and the sun comes out again. Sometimes the fog rolls into the valley and stays there for two to three weeks. People don't see the sun. The sun is always there, they just can't see it. So I was really looking forward to getting up into the foothills and seeing the blue sky and the bright sun.

I stopped in the town of North Fork at the post office and asked directions. The lady there knew exactly whom I was talking about. "Oh, yeah. Cleo, the angel lady. She's got pictures and statues of angels all over the place."

It wasn't hard to find her house. She lived about two miles out of North Fork, off an old dirt road. As I pulled into her driveway, I saw this older woman standing at the door. Have you ever met someone you never knew before, but they had such a warmth and glow that you immediately felt safe and secure and totally at home? Well, that's the way it was with this woman, Cleo. Just the way she looked at me, I felt totally safe.

"Come on in. Sit down by the fire and relax," she said. "I've been waiting for you."

For some reason I wasn't surprised.

"Just sit down over here. Close your eyes and listen. Feel free to ask questions about whatever you like. Because I'm gonna tell you the truth about angels. You don't have to take any notes or tape record anything," she assured me. "Just open your mind and listen. You will remember everything I'm going to tell you." This is what she said:

"There are many dimensions in the universe. We do not live in a physical universe. We live in a spiritual universe. You and I are presently occupying the time-space dimension called planet Earth. It is not the only dimension there is.

"There are many dimensions inhabited by different kinds of souls. Some of these souls are known as angels. There are basically two kinds of angels: Guardian angels and Archangels. Guardian angels sometimes inhabit the Earth, and you really can't tell them from other ordinary people. Guardian angels also act like windows to the other dimensions. They come along every now and then to help us open our minds so we can catch a glimpse of the larger spiritual universe.

"Here is what you have to remember about guardian angels. People will feel and see them according to their own belief system and according to how these people view the world, the universe, and God. There will never be agreement on exactly who these angels are and what they do, because the people describing them will have different belief systems, and, therefore, different perceptions.

"I have had direct experience with angels. I communicate with them. I know them. And you may also have an experience with them if you really desire to. But your experience will be different from mine. So go ahead and ask me as many questions as you like."

"Where do angels come from?" I asked. "Are they real, or are they just ideas in mind?"

"Angels come from the same place that human beings come from," Cleo answered. "They come from God. They are made out of God. Angels are very real. They have individual personalities, but they do not have bodies like you and I, although an angel may take on a body and look very human. There are millions and millions of guardian angels immediately surrounding the Earth. In fact, every human being has at least one guardian angel. The main function of guardian angels is to watch over the person and to help in times of trouble, if they can."

"What do you mean if they can?" I inquired.

"Well, powers of guardian angels are limited. They can help guide and direct human behavior, but they will not interfere with free will. Let me give you an example. Let's say you're driving along the road in the fog and you lose your way and you're about to hit a tree. An angel can intervene and help in some way to prevent an accident or make sure that you won't be hurt. An angel can protect you from natural catastrophe and help you to become aware about an event.

Sometimes, the angel can be that still small voice within you warning you to do or not do a particular thing.

"Some humans can actually see guardian angels. Others can only feel them. But in order for an angel to help, people must be open to the possibility that they can be helped.

"Now, for example, if a person were to pull a gun on you and try to shoot you, your guardian angel could not interfere. The reason is because the guardian angel can not interfere with the free will of an individual human being. Do you see the difference?" Cleo asked.

"Yeah. I guess," I said. "In other words, where human beings are involved and making decisions, the angel can't help you."

"That's almost it," she said. "But, for example, in an automobile accident, there might be two or more people involved. But if the other person does not intend to cause you injury, then the angel is not violating the law of free will and can, if the person is open, help alleviate or minimize the accident. But if people intend to hurt you, the angel cannot interfere with their free will."

"How do angels minimize an accident?" I asked.

"It's very simple," she said. "Angels function in more than one dimension. And so they can, through focused intention, manipulate time and space. They can actually move objects around.

"Again, using our original example, a car might be headed directly towards a tree. At the last second, the focused intention of an angel might intervene and push the car either to the right or left and thus avoid the tree, or they might slow down the car. A lot of this depends upon the ability of the particular angel."

"You mean guardian angels have different abilities?" I asked.

"Oh, yes. Guardian angels are like human beings in some ways," Cleo answered. "Some simply have greater talents than others. It's part of the evolutionary process. Your guardian angel is basically a reflection or mirror of your consciousness."

"Wow. I'm starting to get confused," I said.

"Just hang in there," she said. "It will become more and more clear to you. Just remember everything and everyone is interconnected. What you do affects everyone else, including your guardian angel."

"What else do guardian angels do?" I asked.

"If you are open to them, they can give you insight," Cleo answered. "They can give you guidance and direction. They can act like a catalyst to open the energy systems of your body so that you can vibrate with a higher energy. But, remember, in order for your guardian angel to really help you, you must be open to it."

"Why do you say 'it' ?" I asked. "Don't guardian angels have sex?"

"Do you mean are they male and female?" she chuckled. "Guardian angels have what we call a 'psycho-noetic body.' This 'psycho-noetic body' is neither male nor female. The word you would use is 'androgynous'. When humans see an angel, they see it according to their perception. Then the angel may take on a male or female shape. They don't have a male or female gender per se."

"Do they have sex?" I asked.

"Well, they don't have sex the way human beings have sex," she answered. "But they do merge with one another. They have the ability to merge with their psycho-noetic bodies. They have time to be with each other, according to your perception of time, mostly when human beings are sleeping. Therefore, guardian angels form friendships and groups and discuss their lives just like human beings discuss their lives here on Earth."

"Well, why do guardian angels help some people and not others? Lots of times people are in accidents and are killed or severely injured," I said.

"That's right," she said. "Remember, a guardian angel can only help you if you are open to the possibility. Also remember that guardian angels reflect the consciousness of the human being they are around. Human beings function at different levels of consciousness. Some people are manipulative. Some people are just plain mean. Other people are loving. At their essence, guardian angels are not manipulative or mean, but their bodies will reflect that vibration from the human being. In other words, they may not be able to help a person unless he or she is functioning at a high enough level of consciousness."

"What about little children?" I asked. "Why wouldn't they help little children?"

"Who says they don't?" Cleo said. 'Many times guardian angels help little children. Human adults often think little children are not aware, but many times they are aware. They actually talk to their angels. They play with them, sing with them. I'm sure your guardian angel helped you when you were little."

"I don't remember that," I said.

"I'm sure you will," said Cleo, looking at me with a sense of knowingness.

"Do angels have wings?" I asked.

"Actually, no, they don't," Cleo answered. 'The idea of wings came from human beings. When humans saw angels, they saw them according to their perceptions. And some humans perceived wings on the angels. Actually, wings aren't necessary for angels, because they don't need them to fly. They simply transport themselves from one location to another instantaneously by intention."

"Where did the idea of wings come from," I asked.

"The idea of wings actually came from the Catholic Church," answered Cleo. "It wasn't even lawful to depict or draw angels in art until after the eighth century. People who had seen angels knew that they moved from one place to another, and so artists, in order to depict movement, relied on racial memories of the Greek gods, like Hermes, who was the messenger to the other gods. They copied the wings of other winged creatures like Nike, the Greek symbol of victory, and Eros, the god of love. People in history saw wings, because angels appeared to them in ways that corresponded with the thoughts of the people. Angels want people to be comfortable seeing them. The wings made them look peaceful. Angels will look a certain way to you, because that is what your eyes expect. But they really don't have wings."

"Do human beings ever become angels?" I asked.

"It is possible that a human being can become an angel if that is the desire of the human being as part of evolutionary growth. Human beings have three bodies: a physical body, a mental body, and a spiritual body. Angels have two bodies, a mental body and a spiritual body. When a human being dies to the physical world, it leaves its physical body. The Bible has stated this correctly when it says that the body returns to dust and the soul returns to God. Every death involves a rebirth. A human may choose to live in the dimension of angels and thus become a guardian angel. But no human being ever becomes an Archangel. And no guardian angel ever becomes an Archangel. This is because there are qualitative differences between guardian angels and Archangels. But it is possible for a human being to become a guardian angel, if that is truly the deep desire of the human."

"Okay," I said. "What about food? What do angels eat?" I asked.

"They don't eat anything," Cleo said. "You must understand the purpose of food. The purpose of food on Earth is to help give energy to people. All food is stored energy or secondary energy. Angels don't need food because they receive their energy directly from God. Because humans live in a world of time and space, in a physical dimension, they have the capacity to convert other physical energy systems to energy that they use for their bodies. Vegetables are energy systems, fruits are energy systems, and animals are energy systems. All the human does when he eats vegetables, fruit, or meat, is to convert the energy contained in these systems to energy that he can use."

"This brings up the question of vegetarianism," I said. "Are human beings supposed to eat meat, or just fruit and vegetables?"

"The problem with your question," Cleo said, "are the words 'supposed to'. Let's put it this way. For some humans, it is more helpful if they do not eat meat because it is harder for their systems to metabolize the meat into the energy necessary for their growth. However, other humans can and do eat meat, and their metabolism is unaffected. So it is very difficult to make a generalization here. If you are really interested in this area, I would suggest that you take a period of about three months and eat only fruits and vegetables during this time. See if you feel better, have more energy, and harmonize more with life. If you do, you should probably stick with vegetarianism. Fruits and vegetables are easier to metabolize than meat. And it is true that fish, turkey and chicken are easier to metabolize than red meat. But, some people can metabolize red meat and receive just as much energy as if they ate fruit and vegetables. Only individual experimentation can give you that answer.

"Humans are energy systems made of light and intelligence. Angels are energy systems made of light and intelligence. Archangels are a totally different kind of energy system. But, still, they are made of light and intelligence. All of these systems need a continuing source of energy to grow and evolve, with the exception of the Archangels, who are not subject to evolution. They are simply Divine Essences that surround the Earth. Archangels receive a continuing pure, clear source of energy from God, the Source of all energy. Angels receive the same energy in a more diluted form from the Archangels. In one way, human beings are unique from the angels and Archangels. Human beings obtain energy from three sources.

"The first source of energy is God or Spirit, generated through the Archangels. The second source is food or stored energy, and the third source is energy transferred from other human beings. Oh, yes. There is one other source. People who have pets often receive spiritual energy that is transferred from the pet to the human. That is why it is important for people, especially people who live alone, to have a pet."

"What about all these other kinds of angels that I've heard about? I think they're called seraphim and cherubim in the Bible?" I asked.

"Yes," Cleo said. "That's right. They are in the Bible and in a lot of other documents, too. That is part of the mythology about angels created by human beings. I repeat to you, there are only two kinds of angels: Archangels and guardian angels. The Archangels may be seen as divine generators of God energy. The other angels may be seen as individualized energy systems that help human beings in their evolutionary process.

"The idea of seraphim and cherubim came from the Babylonians. Originally, a cherub was considered to be a cross between a mammal and a giant bird. A seraph was a flying serpent with six wings and four faces."

"What about all these hierarchies of angels that were described in *Paradise Lost*?" I asked.

"Milton, as well as Dante before him, got much of his information from an apocryphal book called *The Book of Enoch*. But this is all part of mythology and has no basis in reality. For example, there is another apocryphal book titled *Jubilees*, written around 135 B.C. that states that the angels were created by God on the first day. They were called watchers, who descended to Earth to instruct the children of men on righteousness. And according to the *Book of Jubilees*, angels ate manna, the nectar of the Gods.

"But, in fact, angels were not created on the first day," Cleo continued. "All creation, including all life, occurred instantaneously. The discovery of God's creation appears as evolution, but that has to do with the rules of time and space. But there is only one creation. Everything that ever has been in existence or ever will be in existence is already in existence. Everything you need or will ever need has already been given to you. The gift has already been given. It's all here, it's all now, just waiting for your discovery.

"Two of the greatest human sources on the history of angels are Dionysius and St. Thomas Aquinas. Both of their discussions, which formed the foundation of our knowledge about angels, are drawn from logic, the reading of different scriptures, and hearsay. They are not based on personal experience. It was Dionysius who named the order of angels in Heaven. You can read all about these hierarchies and orders, but they have nothing to do with the way the universe actually works."

"But I thought there were good angels and bad angels," I said. "I thought there were angels, demons, and fallen angels?"

Cleo turned and looked at me with an expression of deep compassion and love. "The idea of fallen angels," she said, "was first proposed by Enoch in the 2nd century B.C. His work was actually suppressed from the Bible. It is here where the story of the fallen angels originates. According to Enoch, there were two hundred angels called the 'Watchers or the Awake Ones', who rebelled against God. The rest of the angels stayed up in Heaven and obeyed God. These two hundred descended because, among other reasons, they wanted to have sex with the daughters of men. They also wanted to impart secrets to human women, whom they would marry, secrets about magic and plants, medicine, weapons, and many other things, the secrets of the universe.

"The *Book of Enoch* is an attempt to explain how evil got to the Earth. To explain evil, Enoch developed this theory and the myth of fallen angels. You see, one of the purposes for a human to incarnate on planet Earth is the learn to take responsibility and dominion. But many people do not want to take responsibility for their actions, so they embrace ideas of fallen angels, a devil, or a Satan. This is one of the greatest escape mechanisms ever invented, and it is also a technique to assuage guilt. In reality, there are no fallen angels, and there never have been. There are no demons, and there are no devils, except in the creation of human imagination."

"What about Lucifer?" I asked. "Isn't Lucifer really Satan?"

Cleo answered, "No, Lucifer and Satan are two totally different characters and originate historically from separate myths. Let's take Lucifer first.

Lucifer, in angel mythology, is the Angel of Light. The original intent of the story of Lucifer was to convey the same idea that is contained in the Greek story of Narcissus. The purpose of light is to shine. When you receive light, you are to give it away. Lucifer represents light that tries to contain itself. The result is inversion. The light, turning in on itself, eats away at itself. It attempts to take instead of give. It is a 'false light', leading away from the truth."

"William Blake was absolutely correct when he said that evil is only the deprivation of good. When the human soul emerges from this illusion of evil, Lucifer resumes his original status as one of God's greatest Archangels of Light. We must realize that what was recorded in the past about angels was manipulated to fit with historical theories of the time."

"Historically, Lucifer represents the human quest for enlightenment. Lucifer is the Angel of Light associated with the planet Venus. According to one historical myth, God is very jealous and does not want humanity to have knowledge. So, when Lucifer tries to give Light to humanity, God gets very mad and kicks him out of Heaven. But in truth, Lucifer is only a projection of our own negativity, based on our own sense of separation from God."

"We need to distinguish between books about angels and direct experience with angels. Much of the history of angels is based upon books about angels. If seen in terms of myth and allegory, they make some sense. But they certainly are not to be taken literally."

Cleo then went to her bookshelf and pulled out a very small book. She showed me the cover. It was titled The Secrets of Lucifer. She opened the book and began to read.

ANGEL QUEST

Chapter Four
The Secrets of Lucifer

"I am the Lightbearer. I am the light of the morning star that illuminates the darkness."

ANGEL QUEST

Once upon a time, actually before time, before the planets and the stars, there was just God, and God was alone. "It's no fun being alone," He said. "There is nothing to experience, nothing to feel. There is no life, and, therefore, no joy. And, at that, God said, "Let there be joy."

At that very moment, creation occurred, not just the Earth, but the entire universe, the sun, the moon and the stars.

And the angels were created to be in Heaven with God and mankind was created to be on Earth to live out life in Paradise. And everyone was happy and full of joy.

One day, one of the angels named Lucifer came to see God. He was called the Archangel of Light and was much loved by God. "I've been thinking," Lucifer said to God, "everything is running so smoothly up here in Heaven and down there on Earth. Everyone bows down to you and worships you. All the angels do exactly what you desire. In Paradise on Earth men and women obey you in all ways. Don't you think all this is a little boring? I mean everything is so predictable. You know everything that's going to happen. I suppose you could call it all 'good,' and 'very good', but how do you really know that? I mean, you have nothing to compare it to. Don't you think we need a little variety?"

"I don't think, I know," said God, a little taken back. "I think your light has gone to your head, Lucifer. But I do have to admit it is pretty boring seeing the same thing every day, the angels bowing down and singing my praises and the people down on Earth cavorting in the garden. Do you have any suggestions?"

"What we need to make Heaven and Earth a little more exciting," Lucifer said, "is some variety and drama. Let's introduce some variables here, so we don't know exactly what's going to happen."

"Variables, excitement, drama?", God said, mulling these new ideas over in His Mind. "I suppose we could do all that, but then there's always the danger that part of my creation may feel a sense of separation and get disconnected from me. They might get lost."

"Exactly!" said Lucifer. "And if they get lost, they could get found again, and then you have a perfect game of hide-and-seek. We could hide from the humans and let them find us."

"Well, a game like that would surely break the monotony around here," said God. "Let's do it, but with a few twists. First, we won't tell them it's a game. They'll have to discover that for themselves. Second, we will give them choice. They can choose when and how and in what manner they want to play."

"Sounds like 'free will' to me," said Lucifer, very pleased that his suggestions were being considered by the Almighty One.

"OK, it's done," God said. "Let the games begin."

And they did. With that, humans began to think for themselves. They began to explore places other than the garden. They began to ask questions and debate. Before you knew it, there was variety, diversity and drama.

For the first time, humans could think anything they wanted. They could even think there was no God if they wanted. They experienced whatever they thought and believed it as their reality. And many of them began to feel isolated and separated from God and from one another.

God and Lucifer were amazed by all the intricacies and complications, the pain and sorrow, as well as the joy and happiness. At first, God wasn't sure if He liked this new game. "It's not nearly as orderly as before and in no way as predictable," He said.

"That's true," said Lucifer. "But before, humans loved you unconsciously, without experience, without choice. They loved you as the animals do. By introducing our game, you are creating a superior kind of species, a species of beings who come to a conscious understanding of life, who decide to love you of their own free will. Now that's the kind of love worth having. No more bowing and scraping unconsciously, but a coming into the awareness of a deep communion with you. That's so much more precious. Out of all the things in your vast creation, human beings, consciously and with all of their heart, choose to love you.

When Lucifer was finished talking, God had to agree. "Yes," He said, "we have created a very precious thing here: a human being with the capacity to find and experience love in a very conscious way. And

I know that in their own time and way everyone will eventually find this love."

"What will we do then?" asked Lucifer.

"Well, I suppose we could start the whole thing over again," God answered. "But let's not think about that now."

"I just got another idea," Lucifer said. "Do you mind if I ask you something?"

"What's on your mind, Lu?" asked God, by now feeling quite good about the turn of events, for life had become exciting, unpredictable and very interesting.

"Don't you think it would only be fair to give the angels the power of choice like the humans? Then we could consciously decide to love you, too."

"That's true," God said. "But if I give you the gift of free will, you could also choose not to love me. You could choose to disobey me. You could get lost. Do you want to take that chance?"

"If I don't," Lucifer said, "then I am forever an observer of life and not an active participant. Now, it is fun to watch. But I think I would rather play. And if I fall, I will live. And if I live, I will learn. And if I learn, I will find my way back to you."

"Well," said God, "you are my favorite angel, if I had a favorite angel, and I will miss your companionship. Most of all, I think I will miss your crazy ideas. But angels should have the right to choose just like humans. The same logic that applies to their learning to consciously love, should also apply to you. So, yes, go ahead. Have free will. Join in the game. But don't get too lost."

When God uttered these words, Lucifer began to glow. His light began to shine brighter than all the other angels'. "Thank you, thank you, thank you," he said, "for allowing me to play." And with that, he consciously fell over backwards, kind of like a backflip, and tumbled from Heaven.

The game was now complete. God, The Divine Observer, watched. Some angels followed Lucifer. Over time, the role of these 'fallen angels' became clearer. They provided contrast for human choices. Mankind had to be presented with the good and bad, the right and wrong. It could be said that Lucifer's function was to provide a rich and diverse background for human choices. Some humans called this background evil. Some made up stories about Lucifer, and then believed the stories. That was their choice, and it made the game even richer and more diverse. Other angels decided to stay with God to help the game by leaving clues here and there for humankind. These angels were the messengers from God, who would visit humans when God thought that maybe they were getting a little too lost and needed a little help.

And this leads to the question, who is the seeker and who is the finder? Is God seeking us, or are we finding God? But one thing is certain: Angels are participating in the game, each with its own role. Some say Lucifer and his angels try to tempt mankind, to pull man's thoughts away from God. But that really misunderstands Lucifer's role. He plays the game to help humans in their choosing. If you're gonna have right, you gotta have wrong. There's always gonna be light and dark as long as the game is played.

Will the game ever end? And what happens then? Who knows? As God said, "Let's not think about that now

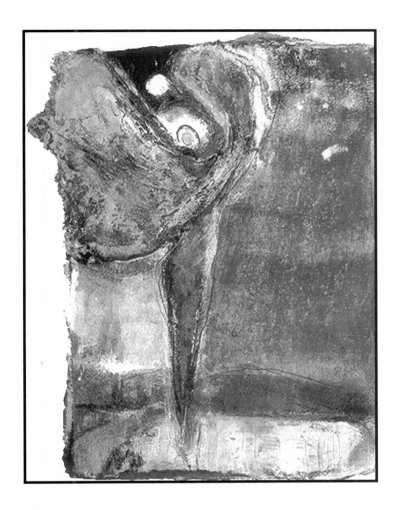

Chapter Five
Angels and Archangels

"We greet you with profound love and light. We are here to help guide you on your journey towards wholeness." As you walk with us, know that you are loved with an everlasting love."

ANGEL QUEST

"Wow," I said. "I've never read or heard of a story about Lucifer like that before. That makes a lot of sense."

Cleo smiled. "So depending on whose mythology you're reading, Lucifer can be interpreted in a number of different ways. But it is really historically inaccurate to equate him with Satan. I suppose you want me to clear up the confusion."

"Please," I said.

"The term Satan can be traced back to the ancient Persian royal courts. Satan didn't refer to a person, it referred to an officer of the King. The word "satan" in Persia meant "the eyes and ears of the king." Just as it was the job of the court jester to make the King laugh, so it was the job of the Satan to go around the towns and villages of the kingdom to check on how the people were doing and then report back to the king. Sometimes "the satan" had to bring bad news to the king. Sometimes he had to present arguments to the king on behalf of the people. Over the years, myths and stories grew up about "the satan". Some said "satan" would go into the villages and stir up trouble among the people just so he would have some juicy gossip to report to the king. Others saw "satan" as the "adversary to the king, always painting the bleakest picture of the happenings in the kingdom. At any rate the term came to have a negative connotation and "satan" came to be know as a good for nothing trouble maker.

So, when the Jewish prophets in exile begin to try to describe the heavenly court of the Almighty King it was natural to use earthly analogies. Since "satan" was an officer of the Persian kingdom, he became an officer of the Heavenly court. At first "Satan" was considered the eyes and the ears of God, but as more ideas of duality crept into later Judaism, Satan became an adversary to God and a personification of evil. After all, somebody has to take the blame when things go wrong.

"Satan" never was an angel. He became equated with Lucifer by St. Augustine and other early Christian writers, through another series of myths to explain the nature of evil. The greatest mischief done on this planet is by those who perpetuate these myths. As I said before, it distracts people from the real cause of evil, human igno-rance. But it is not you purpose to dwell on negativity. I'm here to tell you about the truth about angels.

"Did you know that only three angels are actually named in the Old Testament? And one of these, Raphael, is found in the Catholic Book of Tobit. The other two are Michael and Gabriel.

"You indicated you've heard of the hierarchy of angels. Well, that came from Enoch, whom I've already mentioned. He told about his travels to Heaven and learning about the angels.

"So historically, the three great influences of angels were: Enoch, Dionysius, 6th century A.D., who named the nine orders of angels, and St. Thomas Aquinas, with his fourteen treatises on angels. All of these are theories about angels and, mostly, are theories about theodicy."

"What is theodicy?" I asked.

"Theodicy is an attempt to explain the riddle of good and evil," Cleo answered. "You see, if God is good and everything is created by God, then everything must be good, including the Earth and all its inhabitants. Well, if this is true, then why does it sometimes feel like 'everything's going to hell in a hand basket'? This good and glorious system of God has to break down in some way. Something runs amok. Certainly, we can't blame the breakdown on God, so we have the story of the fallen angels."

"There are actually nine different historical stories that explain why angels fell. The bottom line of most of these stories is that evil was brought into the world by the angels that fell from Heaven. But even if you study and believe these stories, you still have the question of why God allowed all this to happen in the first place."

"So, you want to know the truth?" Cleo asked. "There are not and there never have been fallen angels. Human beings just don't want to take responsibility for their own actions, so they create the idea of the devil or "satan". If there is evil stuff going on in the world, and there sure is, it is the product of human ignorance. Stories about the devil only compound the ignorance. It is time to grow up and teach people that they are responsible for their own actions, their own lives, and for the life of this planet. There is no good and evil in a universal sense. We have invented it in our own minds by separating ourselves from our spiritual source. So it's time to end all of this nonsense and suffering that's been going on. One way we can do this is by asking the true angels for help."

"Wait a minute," I said. "I've read about a lot of people who have seen demons. Some even claim to have seen the Devil himself. These demons are very real to them. They are not just the product of someone's imagination."

Cleo looked at me rather playfully, "You're absolutely right. They are real to the people who see them. But it doesn't mean they have ultimate reality. Human beings have a marvelous capacity to perceive their own projections. I am not saying that individual people create demons. But I am saying that the idea of demons and the devil exists in what is called the collective unconscious. And when these ideas are illuminated with energy, they seem to take on a life of their own, but they are not real.

"They are simply ideas based on a human attempt to understand how the universe works. That is why I have said that stories dwelling on the ideas of the devil only compound ignorance and keep us from growing spiritually. The devil or demons will never come into the mind of a person who focuses on God and good and love. So the best way not to get caught up in this negativity is to simply avoid giving any of your attention or focus to these ideas."

"Okay," I said. "I understand that if you give your energy to certain ideas, those ideas can become a kind of reality. And maybe that is the way demons are created. But wouldn't that also hold true for angels? Aren't angels just ideas in the minds of people? By focusing on angels, aren't we giving them a reality? What is real and what isn't?"

Cleo looked at me and chuckled. "You came here," she said, "to ask about angels. Now you want a philosophical discussion on the nature of reality. Philosophers have been trying to figure this out since the dawn of time. Let me answer you this way. Do you think you're real?"

"Yes, of course," I answered. "I'm real. I have an identity. I know who I am. I have a continuity of memory."

"Okay," Cleo said. "Now let's assume you have died to your physical body. Would you still be real?"

"Well, I guess so. That would depend on the existence of an afterlife. If we are not just human beings, but immortal spiritual beings, then my reality would have to extend beyond my physical body."

"Exactly," Cleo said. "Your sense of identity is not extinguished at physical death. It is carried on through your psycho-noetic body. You are real and will always have divine individuality. But, demons and mythological creatures and devils have no independent significance. They depend totally upon the perception of a sentient being. Sentient beings exist whether or not there is anyone to perceive them. But even sentient beings can only exist within God. Just as human beings give life to ideas that they create by focused attention, so does God, the ultimate source of all life, give life to the ideas of His creation."

"Well, if I get your drift," I said, "you're telling me that if something comes from God, it is real. But if it comes secondarily, from the mind of humans, it does not have ultimate reality."

"That's it," she said. "And as for angels, they are emanations from the Mind of God, and, therefore, they have an innate reality to them. But, as I've said, there is a fundamental difference between angels and Archangels. Where angels move around and communicate with humans on Earth, Archangels do not."

"Tell me more about Archangels," I said.

"All right," Cleo said. "There are seven Archangels. Archangels are like energy vortexes, emanating from the Central Source, God, or what is sometimes called the Unified Field. Each Archangel represents one of the seven directions. Michael from the north, stands for Power. Uriel, from the south, stands for Beauty. Raphael, from the west, stands for Wisdom. Camael, from the east stands for Joy. Gabriel, from the within, stands for Love. Aneal, from below, stands for Life. Metatron, from above, stands for Light. These Archangels have one purpose only. They are to send energy to Earth in the form of spiritual prototypes or patterns. They exist exclusively to serve humanity and the Earth. When humans open themselves to enough energy from one Archangel, they merge with that Archangel. As a result, the person then embodies the quality or essence of the Archangel.

"All people have seven energy systems within their psycho-noetic body that correspond to the seven Archangels. When they merge with all seven Archangels, their entire consciousness is transformed, and they become their spiritual potential. That is, they begin to manifest and live their full potential as spiritual beings on the Earth."

"This seems awfully incredible," I said.

"It is incredible," Cleo said. "You have to understand universal energy. Energy is made up of light and intelligence. And in its unmanifest form, it is simply potential. The Archangels are vast energy systems that particularize the universal energy into divine prototypes. The result of this particularization is life on planet Earth."

"That would imply," I said, "that there might be other Archangels for other planets or other universes."

"Yes," Cleo said. "But what I am revealing to you does not explain how the entire universe works. You see, the universe works on a need-to-know basis. Your individual destiny and the destiny of the planet Earth will be revealed to you, but not your ultimate destiny. Because that is simply incomprehensible to you at this time. It's like trying to explain quantum physics to five-year-olds. They may understand a little, but they're really not interested. You can only truly know about something that you can do something about. You have come to this planet to learn how to love, and that means to live harmoniously with your self, with others, with the planet, with the angels and with God. Speculations about other planets and other universes and how the whole system works are just that, speculation. Knowledge is revealed to you when you can apply it.

"If your desire is deep enough, you will be given additional information to help prepare the planet for the coming transformation."

"Wow," I said. "This is almost too much."

"There's more," Cleo assured me. "Every time one human being merges with one Archangel, that is, fully opens his energy system, aligning himself with the energy vortex of the Archangel, one thousand new angels are awakened. These angels are an actual product of the merging of the Archangel and the human being. They in turn move out to other people to help quicken and awaken them. The more people are awakened to their spiritual nature, the greater the chances for future merging, until the entire consciousness of the planet Earth is illumined. When enough people merge with all seven Archangels, a quantum shift will take place on the Earth. This is what has been called the transformation, the kingdom of Heaven on Earth.

"The truth about Archangels is that it is their purpose to serve the Earth and humanity. It is not their purpose to praise and glorify God. God, the Supreme Light and Intelligence, out of which everything is created, does not seek or need praise or glory.

"There has been a real misunderstanding throughout history concerning the word worship. Its true meaning is not to bow down before or to supplicate. It means to commune with. Human beings are to worship God by communing with these divine or spiritual vortices emanating from God. This is the true meaning of worship. 'I am the Person that Thou art and Thou art the Person that I am.' You learn to receive universal love energy. And once you receive this divine energy of love, it begins to open your energy systems more and more, so you can give this energy away.

"Human beings are not here to worship the angels or Archangels. You are to communicate with the angels and open yourself to the Archangels by invoking the Essence of the particular Archangel and asking it to come to you."

Cleo walked over by the fireplace. For about thirty seconds she didn't speak. She seemed to be waiting for me to absorb all that she told me. Then she turned and said, "I have told you that these seven Archangels correspond to energy systems found in the human body. In a real sense, because these energy systems are somewhat open in all people, you have already been unconsciously communing with the Archangels. But the time has come to become consciously aware of who you are, to speed up your evolution by fully opening your energy centers. The conscious merging with each Archangel will help you to do this.

"It is no coincidence that you came here. Your unconscious desires have led you to this place. Your deep desire for spiritual knowledge has helped bring you here. You see, your mind really is open. You have come to the intellectual awareness that the universe is made up of one essence, one energy, appearing as light. You sense that everything is light. You are beginning to get the feeling that everything is sacred and holy. In the last three or four years, your prayer-meditation groups have helped you become aware of these things. Now is the time to experience what you believe. You have asked with an open heart to know the truth about angels, and your request is now being granted."

As she said these things to me, I felt her energy moving into my body. She was not only reading my mind; She was reading my heart. I actually began to feel the tears well up in my eyes. This is the beginning, I thought to myself. This is the beginning of all that I've hoped for and desired. All that I thought was lost to me is being revealed. And I felt such a deep sense of gratitude and caring, it was almost as if my heart was starting to break. Again she read my mind as she looked at me with total compassion and love. "Don't worry about your heart beginning to break," she said. "It will break, and when it breaks, it will break open. And then you will be able to receive even more and more love. Just remember, you are the beloved."

"Why do I feel such a connection and closeness to you?" I asked.

"We are kindred souls," she answered. "We have journeyed through the stars together. We have all come from the same Central Source. Remember, there is only one creation. It came about in one instance, every soul, everything, and everyone was created at the same instant. But not everything and everyone appeared in form at the same time. There are forms and manifestations that have not yet made their appearance. Angels weren't created first. But Archangels appeared first before there was life on this planet. These Archangels, and energy vortexes are like huge generators of life force, affecting the planet, and bringing life to it."

Suddenly, a line from a poem popped into my head:

"Out of the muck and mire of things,
something sings."

She read my mind again. "That's right," she said. "And the first songs were the voices of the Archangels. Their sound created the planet Earth and all life on it. And if you listen real closely, you can hear them singing today."

For the first time all day, I looked out the window and noticed the fog. It was getting dark, and I realized that I had sat totally enthralled with this woman Cleo for six straight hours.

She must have sensed a bit of concern on my face, for she said, "Yes. It's time that you get back to the valley before the fog becomes too thick. Don't worry. You will be able to access all the information that I have given you. All you have to do is ask."

As I stood up, she came towards me and gave me one of the most wonderful hugs I've ever had. I felt her total and unconditional love, and knew that I was in the presence of a very special person.

"I can't thank you enough," I said. "This has been one of the most important days of my life."

"That's what happens," she answered, "when you start wanting to know the truth about angels. And as you continue your journey, just remember, wherever you go and whatever you do, the angels go with you."

I walked out the door of her cabin, turned and waved. I saw her standing in front of the cabin as I began to slowly wind my way down the dirt road and back to Fresno. The fog had become much thicker. I immediately put my headlights on low beam, wishing that I had fog lights on my car. This is gonna be a slow ride, I thought to myself. I might as well just sit back and relax.

As I passed through the town of North Fork, visibility was no more than fifty feet. I felt cars passing me, coming the other way, and they sounded more like the wind than cars. All noises seemed muffled. I rolled down my windows so I could get a better feel for the road. The mist was quickly settling on my windshield. This is almost scary, I thought to myself. Then, suddenly, I saw bright lights directly in front of me. The thought that flashed through my mind was 'a semi-truck and trailer on the wrong side of the road.' I knew there would be an impact. I swerved to the right. Then everything went black.

ANGEL QUEST

Chapter Six

My Guardian Angel Appears

"Come into the Light and I will comfort you. I will surround you with love and transform you fear into a great and abiding faith. The Universe and all the angels have been eagerly awaiting for the revelation of the sons and daughters of God. You are that revelation."

The fog. The lights. The truck. The blackness of it all. And then the starry sky. The tunnel of light. The experience of overwhelming light and sound. Is this what it means to die? I thought I was just beginning to find my purpose on Earth. And I was just starting to like my body better, all that dieting, gone to waste. All that working out at the gym. And then, the thought just popped into my head, or my consciousness, "That's life. And this is life. And it's the same life, whether it's here or there, I still have a sense of identity, I am still me. I just don't know what this me is."

But, in the reality of the light, I felt so much alive. It felt so real to me, like my life on Earth was a sleep-walking illusion. Is this what it means to wake up? This mingling and this merging. Where did I end and where did the light begin? "I am the light. I am the love. I am the sound." This must be what the mystics felt when they attempted to describe the cosmic experience. Words could never capture this experience. Even to call it an experience implies some subject-object relationship, when in truth I was experiencing only unity, only the One. And yet, it was still unity in relationship. "I am the One speaking to the One, but I still have a sense of individuality, a sense of identity. I am All, and I am the individual, both at the same time. 'Both-and', confusing to the relative mind, delightful to the soul."

As the light began to speak to me, or more properly, commune with me, I felt the last vestiges of fear leave me. I felt totally at peace, totally at home. I was being embraced by an overwhelming love. For the first time, I spoke. Or at least I think I spoke. It felt funny, but apparently my thoughts were communicated. "'Who are you, and where are we, and what in the world is happening?" I asked, all at once.

The voice in the light said, "I am your angel. You are in a dimension different from that of Earth. And nothing in the world is happening to you, because you are not there. You're just beginning to go through a different experience of livingness."

"My angel?" I asked. "You mean like my guardian angel?"

"Yes. That's right," the light replied. "That is the label that humans have put on us. I am the reminder of who you are, who you really are. I am here to remind you of your divine potential and to tell you about it. I guard you, I guide you, and I watch over you."

"What's your name?" I inquired.

"We don't have names. But you have named me, so I have taken on that name for your convenience."

"Then how come I don't remember your name?"

"You do," said the angel. "You just have to remember back to the time when you believed I was real."

"I don't know what you're talking about."

"Yes, you do," said the angel. "Do you remember when you were a little boy, and you had an imaginary friend who you used to play with? Most children had imaginary friends when they were little. Well, that was me. That was us. We were there, and we did play with you. We were with you. What was the name of your imaginary friend?"

Suddenly, I remembered. "Jack!" I said. "My imaginary friend was Jack. That's what I named him. I have no idea why I named him Jack. I hope it was okay."

The angel laughed. Yes, laughed. I felt his laughter.

"It's not important what you named me. I accepted the name. It felt strong and powerful. When you were four years old, you wanted to name me Jack. That was okay with me. And if you wanted to make me a male angel, that was all right, too."

"Well, are you a male angel?" I asked.

"I am now," he said. "Basically, I take on the form, the gender, or the body that you want to see." As he began to say these things, I began to see a form in the light, a being of light, all shiny and ethereal, sort of half opaque and half transparent.

"I see you," I said. "Do you have wings?'"

"Do you want me to have wings?" he asked. "They're really not necessary. We can appear, disappear, and be wherever we want to, whenever we want to."

"Okay," I said. 'No wings. But I would like to see your face and touch your hand."

"No problem," he replied. "I'll be right next to you, and you can touch my hand any time you want." The moment he said that, his form moved closer to me, still illuminating all over, but with distinguishable features. He appeared to be a very strong, self-assured angel.

"Are you ready?" he asked.

"'Ready for what?'" I said.

"Well, you didn't actually pray to know everything we are going to show you. But you did ask to know more about angels, and your motives are pure. At some level, your request is more than curiosity. You sense that there is something to this angel business, and you want to know more. At a much deeper level you are asking: 'Is there a way that knowing about angels can help humans on Earth? Can this knowledge help people live better and more fulfilled lives?' The answer to these questions is 'yes'. Angels can help you. We have a message for you. And by understanding the truth about angels, you can help make a difference on your planet."

"So, are you ready to begin?" he said.

"This is too overwhelming," I answered. "You want me to be a messenger to others? Why don't you just send an angel down to tell the people what you want them to hear?"

"We don't want you to be a messenger. You want to be the messenger. Through your deep desire, you picked us. And, it's one thing to give people guidance and intuition through angels, but it's quite another thing for one human to communicate to another. Let's just say it's easier and more efficient for a human to communicate with humans. They have a little more credibility than angels. So, remember what I said, 'Don't be afraid. There is nothing to fear, ever. I'm here to help you, to guide you, and to nurture you. I have always been with you, and I will never desert you. Touch that desire deep inside you.' Are you ready?"

I heard a force and a power from the depths of me say, 'Yes! Yes!' I touched his hand and I said, "Okay, let's go."

ANGEL QUEST

Chapter Seven

The Orientation

"The Energy of God fills the whole universe. From the beginning, and even before the beginning, there is the Mind of God. There is nothing outside this Mind. It permeates all things in It. It permeates the Archangels, the angels, and all people. God's Essence is everywhere."

Instantaneously we were in a class room with people. There must have been over a hundred people, and along side each person was an angel. The people were dressed in casual clothes and looked very human and very real. The angels were in white robes. Just then, what appeared to be another angel in a violet robe, came into the room. "You may be seated," she said. "Listen very closely. You will need this information when the time comes." We all sat down, and she began to speak.

"You are here because of an honest desire to help bring transformation to the planet. To do this, you'll need some background on how human beings think. Humans grow through different stages of awareness.

"The first stage is called the 'Victim Stage.' They see themselves as victims of outer conditions that they cannot control. Conditions, people, and events have independent significance and things 'just happen.' The world is a scary place and it's better not to take chances. If they succeed, they are lucky, and if they fail, it is fate. They look for 'their good' outside of themselves. They attempt to establish their self-esteem in groups and in other people. They are willing to give up their personal independence and freedom to 'somebody who knows all the answers.' They become true believers. They see life as survival and often they feel trapped by circumstances, claiming they have no choice. Their dominant emotion is fear.

"Victims see time in terms of commodity. There are beginnings and endings, startings and stoppings, time-in and time-out, time to go to work, time to pick up the kids, time to go to church, and time to punch the clock. They see this 'commodity time' being dictated by some force out there. 'Some external power is doing it to us.'

"In short, victims are coping, groping and moping. But, in the end, they are also hoping. For the victim, hope is the portal of entry into the next stage of awareness. Without hope, there is despair, and they remain in the victim stage. With hope, they are open to the possibility that perhaps there is another way of seeing. So the first thing we must do is give people hope.

"The second stage of awareness is the 'Awakening Stage.' This is a completely experiential, non-conceptual stage. Humans are never awakened by concepts, only by experience. The awakening stage occurs in different ways in different people. It has been described as 'a fleeting glimpse of reality and an unrelenting desire to know the truth.' The 'born again' experience is a real experience and occurs regardless of theology. Theologians get stuck in the conceptual description and think by creating creeds and dogmas, the experience can be recreated. Actually, creeds and dogma help prevent the experience from occurring. When people are truly awakened, they know that there is a reality and an underlying harmony and order in the universe, and they want to know more. The dominant feeling of this stage is excitement, restlessness and discontent with the old ways of living.

"They now begin to recognize a new kind of time, 'organic time.' They begin to feel the rhythm of the universe. They relate more to dawn and dusk, the seasons, their own breathing, their own metabolism. In other words, they start 'to hum inside'.

"The third stage of awareness is called 'Understanding Mind.' This is the meaning of the Bible quotation, 'Be ye therefore transformed by the renewing of your mind.' Humans come to an awareness that they are the creators of their own experience. They understand the statement, 'I'll see it when I believe it.' They discover and apply spiritual laws. They accept the unity of all life, that God is omnipresent, not just somewhere, but equally present everywhere, and that the impersonal law of cause and effect governs the universe. Instead of unconsciously using the Law as a victim, they begin to consciously experiment with it. They begin to realize that their thoughts create their reality. They start to consciously control their thoughts. They come to the realization that they are unique individualizations of God, not separate individuals, but interconnected individualizations. Most important, they come to the knowledge that they are responsible for their life, and they begin to take dominion.

"Worship becomes a meaningful term again. They are not worshipping a force or an entity outside of themselves, but they have an attitude of awe and wonder. They marvel at the grandeur and magnificence of the universe. They are open and receptive to the new. They recognize God in all the details, but at the same time, know that God is beyond and transcends all.

"The fourth stage of awareness is called the 'Embodiment Stage." Jesus said, 'It is done unto you according to your faith.' This means that it is done, not just according to your intellectual understanding, but according to conscious and subjective embodiment. It is not enough to hear truth, to understand truth, or even to accept truth with your conscious mind. You must test it, practice it, until you live it each day.

"The final stage of awareness is called 'Mastership.' Mastership means totally integrating spiritual and human nature into one nature. Masters realize that separation of their spiritual and human nature is only an illusion of mind. They experience a new level of awareness based on unconditional love. They see oneness in everyone and everything. They are Masters of their bodies, their emotions, and their soul. This stage of awareness is not a utopian dream, but a promised reality.

"Aristotle said, 'The true nature of anything is the highest that it can become.' The highest that humans can become is the highest they can conceive. We are here to show you how to bring together Heaven and Earth, how to transform your life and how to see with new eyes and hear with new ears.

With that statement, the angel just disappeared right in front of us. I turned to my guardian angel, Jack. I was full of questions, but he signaled for me to be quiet. I turned my attention back to the front of the room, and another angel dressed in a blue robe appeared and began to speak.

"Listen to the words of Spirit. Open your heart and hear it. This is what Spirit says:

'There is the ineffable, the unmanifest, out of which all manifestation comes, the One, and everything that comes from the One.

Hidden in the mystery of the Universe is this One. Some call it the Presence of God. This Presence is good. Out of the Presence comes Heaven and Earth. Heaven is good. Earth is good. Out of Heaven and Earth come the Archangels, the angels and humans. Everything is connected with the Earth, with Heaven, with the Presence; it is all good.

What is the Presence like? It cannot be described, but it can be experienced. It is a unique and individual experience for each human. It is very real. But the goal is not the experience.

The experience of the Presence is the beginning of awakening to true nature. There is no end. The universe is in harmony and in balance. It is already perfect. We cannot make it better. We cannot improve on what already is. You think you are the observer, somehow on the outside, trying to fix something. You cannot fix something that is not broken. The only distortion is in your way of looking. So stop looking at the Universe like it was some kind of object and start looking with the Universe.

The Energy of God fills the whole universe. From the beginning, and even before the beginning, there is the Mind of God. There is nothing outside this Mind. It permeates all things in it. It permeates the Archangels, the angels, and all people. God's essence is everywhere.

Learn to go to the center of your being. That's where the Presence of God is. That's where peace is. That's where the center of the Universe is. Everything emanates from the inside out. Once you're there at the center, you can look around and see everything. There is stuff and there is the center. Stuff flows out from the center and is constantly moving and changing. The center does not change.

You have chosen to be a part of the human condition on Earth. It's silly to deny it or call it unreal. Take it for what it is. It's part of the process. Once you accept your humanity totally, then you can accept your spirituality. You only get into trouble when you forget who you are, when you identify with 'stuff' rather than Essence, when you see with the eyes of the world rather than the Earth. All you have to do is to remember: You live on the Earth and you Live in the world. The Earth is a harmonious emanation of the One, the

Presence. So are you. In the world, there are opposites. There's good and bad, black and white, here and there, up and down, and it's necessary for meaning in the world. But remember, you are connected with the Earth.

The world is divided into parts and names, too many classifications. It is easy for you to get lost in the particular and the multiplicity of conditions, losing your way in events. But remember the One that is the cause of all of the events.

Do you know what it is like to be at home? The feeling of being at home, at peace, with everything and everyone around you? When you have that feeling of being at home wherever you are, then you know you are connected with all life.

How should you live? Passionate in the process, detached to the outcome. You can't determine the outcome anyway, but you can choose how to live the process. Outcomes aren't real. Feel yourself in the flow of life. Let your soul embrace everyone and everything you meet. Live every second with passion, every minute with desire, every hour with delight, and every day with detachment. Whatever role you choose for today, play it to the fullest.

How do you shine? By letting instead of pushing. By honoring others. By getting outside of yourself. By trusting others and allowing them to experience their own creativity. Avoid calling attention to yourself. You are here to live from the center of peace within you, not from the center of attention. You don't have to prove anything, just be.

Everyone wants magic formulas: how to get rich; how to have right relationships; how to get enlightened. There is no magic formula. There is no method. The only thing a book or a class or a seminar can do is inspire you to find yourself within yourself. How do you look for the ocean when you're swimming in it?

People are always reaching out, always grasping for something else, something to make them feel better, but it won't work. Contentment can only come from inside of you.

You have to face it: You're by yourself. No amount of reaching, grasping, yelling, or screaming is going to change that. Because you don't want to be alone, you surround yourself with people, you structure your time, you try to prevent boredom. But what is yourself? It is a lot more than you think, because it's eternal. It's part of the One, it's life, and it's great, and that's what you are. You will never find contentment until you find yourself, your true self. And how do you find it? Stop looking outside. Stop looking and just be.

Have you thought very much about your own consciousness? Your individual consciousness is the meeting ground of the Universal and the particular. It is the point where God particularizes Itself as you. It is the point of all creativity in you. To 'touch the face of God' is to allow yourself to be open to the possibility. It can only take place in your consciousness.

When you move to the point of God connection in you, where the Universal touches the individual, you arrive at the consciousness of Cause. You can deal with situations before they happen. You can see the order of the Universe and not the confusion. You watch creation unfold in an orderly and beautiful pattern. Others will admire and wonder at your foresight and serenity. There is no need to wonder. You have simply decided to see the Universe from the point of view of First Cause. The higher controls the lower, the inner controls the outer.

You must be very clear about yourself and about the Universe, then you must decide, you must choose, you must establish your purpose in your mind, then you must allow. Simply be open and allow.

When you have a sense of awe and wonder and a real feeling of delight about the mystery of the Universe, you're on your way. Diagrams and concepts are methods, but they are not the way. When you are open with a sense of awe and wonder, when you feel that everything is holy and sacred, you are on your way.

There is no need to prove anything to anyone. There is no need to argue. You cannot make yourself right by making someone else wrong. Just be clear, as clear as you can be, become convicted, then act on your convictions, and God and the angels will take care of the rest.

Take dominion over your life; your body, your mind, your soul, your surroundings, and realize that none of these things are you. Decide and choose without judging. Work without worry. Lead and let at the same time. And don't get too full of anything, especially yourself. See yourself as a container of life, always circulating the contents. You are the vessel, but you must be willing to be emptied in order to be full.

You can't see God because God does not show Itself. God does not seek worship. God doesn't want anything from you. God has already given all of Its Love, Its Power, and Its Presence to you as a gift. All you have to do is discover It, accept It, and use It. From God, through the Archangels, everything comes.

So let it be done unto you. Let people love you. Let life pamper you. Let the Universe come to your aid. Let your angels guide you. It works if you let it. And remember, balance is the key. Make choices, take action, but don't insist on the outcome. Action starts the creative process. Then get out of the way and allow the way to manifest the result .

You never have to be concerned with your friends or your enemies if you're a true friend to yourself. If you know yourself, you will be at home. If you're at home, you will automatically know how to treat others. When you're at home, you treat others with hospitality, with warmth, and with love. Being at home with yourself means you never seek love, never seek acceptance, and never seek approval. You just be you. And everything else takes care of itself.'

The angel stopped speaking, and then all the angels stood up. The people wanted to talk and ask questions, especially questions concerning each other. I looked around the room and my attention fixed upon one person. The thing I noticed was her soft blue eyes. There was a brief moment when her eyes met mine and there was a feeling of recognition, even though I was sure I hadn't seen her before. My guardian angel touched me on the shoulder and signaled for me to remain quiet. We were led out of the room and into a beautiful garden. Each angel directed each person on a particular path. We soon lost sight of each other and I was again alone with my guardian angel. I found myself sitting on a stone bench watching my angel intently.

"What was all that about?" I asked.

"Orientation," answered Jack. "Mandatory orientation. You're not permitted to ask questions during orientation."

"But who were all those people?" I asked.

"People like you. People from your planet going through basically the same experience that you're going through."

"Why couldn't I talk to them?"

"It's not time," explained Jack. "None of you are prepared yet. But you will meet again sometime in the future. But now it's time to move on. Take my hand."

As I touched his hand, we were transported again to a new place.

Chapter Eight

Life After Life

"It's time to take the walk, the journey towards the discovery of your true self, the discovery of your purpose and the discovery of your relationship to the Earth. If you proceed through these doors, there is no turning back. You will join us and become a true messenger, a messenger of the angels, an angel to the angels."

ANGEL QUEST

Suddenly, we were at the entrance of a very large building. It looked like a giant university library. In front of me were two golden doors, about sixteen feet high.

"When these doors open before you, you will actually feel your awareness expanding. You will learn things here that you can take back to Earth to help prepare the people," said the angel.

"Prepare them for what?" I asked.

"For the transformation that is about to take place. Things are changing very rapidly on Earth. There is much disorganization and a great amount of fear. You can help put that fear to rest. But, we're getting ahead of ourselves. It's time to take the walk, the journey towards the discovery, the discovery of yourself, the discovery of your purpose, the discovery of your relationship with the earth. But, there is one thing I must tell you. If you begin this walk, you cannot turn back until you've completed the journey. You will become a different person. Your life will change, and, in many ways, you will be thrown out of your old comfort zones. You will feel a much greater responsibility and love for others. You will become less self-involved. Things will become more ambiguous. What used to be black and white answers will no longer be so, because you will learn the capacity to see and feel from the position of many different people at the same time. You will feel their pain, their anxiety, their fears. We will teach you how to do this. We will teach you how to merge with the consciousness of other sentient beings so that you can know the diversity and complexities of life. For amidst the joys and sorrows of people, you will also know the truth and be able to help guide them towards the truth.

"You may choose right now not to enter this building, not to open these doors, and we will return you to Earth to live out the rest of your natural life. Or, you may choose to become a messenger to help in the coming transformation and to help alleviate fear and suffering on the planet."

As I stood before those doors, I began to reflect on this adventure. "You know," I said, "this whole thing started when I had a desire to know the truth about angels. I didn't realize I was getting into something so much bigger. My questions were relatively simple. I wanted to know where angels come from. What's their purpose? Do they have wings? What do they eat? That sort of thing. And now you're telling me that I'm gonna be some sort of messenger in the cosmic scheme of things. I didn't really sign on for that. Can't I just get the information I want, let it go at that, and get back to my old life?"

"If that's what you want, yes, you can have it," the angel answered. "You can learn all about angels back on Earth. There are lots of books back there on the subject, lots of opinions, lots of perceptions. But, that will always be someone else's view. If you want to know the truth, it has to be the whole truth. You can't peak at reality and be satisfied. There is your old way of doing things and there is God's way. Now, it's not too late to go back to your old way. But if you proceed through those doors, there is no turning back."

"What's on the other side?" I asked. 'I need more information so that I can make some kind of rational decision."

The angel started laughing so hard that I thought he might have a convulsion. "Rational?" he laughed. "Rational? A rational decision is a decision of boundaries, of walls, of containers. It's a decision of limitation. I really would have thought, by now, that you would have extended yourself beyond your pea brain."

"Pea brain?" I exclaimed "I haven't been called that since grade school. I thought you angels had a kinder way of communicating."

"We do, but sometimes we have to use words that you understand to get your attention. Look, we're offering to show you the secrets of the universe to help you with your mission in life, and you are still resisting. Do you know what faith is? Faith is totally trusting this process, totally immersing yourself in life without any knowledge of the outcome. In fact, that is true living. It's the leap beyond the intellect. I know you've already considered that leap or you wouldn't even be here now."

When he said that, I knew he was right. I had always chosen to explore the realm of Spirit, the area beyond the intellect. I had already had spiritual experiences, so, at some level, I already knew that God loved me with an everlasting love and that the entire universe was a holy and sacred creation. I knew the universe was on purpose and that there was a divine plan. And I knew these things, not with my intellect, but with a deeper knowing through both faith and experience.

"Yes, I know that God is Love," I said. "At some level, I have always known it. And you're right. I shouldn't have hesitated."

The angel looked at me with great compassion and said, "And now you can choose to bring that inner knowing into full realization. All you have to say is yes to the rest of your life."

I looked at him with awe and wonderment and uttered the word, "Yes."

He touched me again, and I could feel his love. "I must leave you now," he said. "But, I will never be far away. You may not see me again, but you may feel my presence and hear my voice whenever you ask."

For a few seconds there was silence. I began to see his form turn into light and dissipate. I turned towards the doors, and they opened wide. I saw before me a very large room or a hall. It really did look like a university library, except there were no books and no tables. Material that looked like carpet was under my feet, and I knew that I was supposed to walk down this carpet. It was about three hundred feet long. Down at the other end, I saw what appeared to be an altar.

As I began to walk, immediately the scene changed. Although I kept walking, I was no longer in a room. I was actually in the middle of a life, a life that was so familiar, because it was my life, or rather I should say it was my lives. During this walk, I learned about myself, things I never could have known on a conscious level. My lives kept passing before me. Not only could I observe them, but I could feel them. It was as if I was embodying my whole existence up until the present moment. It was much more than a review or a highlight. It was an actual reliving, but at a tremendously accelerated speed. I saw myself being born, age, and die, only to be born again. I observed that I had had many lives before. But none of these lives, except for my present one, were on the Earth. There were places that looked like the Earth, but I knew they were somewhere else.

Many questions about the journey of the soul and immortality were answered during my walk. Here are some of the things I found out.

Although we have many lives, and there will be many lives to come, we do not always reincarnate back to Earth. We will come back to Earth as long as there is unfinished business. There are other places. These dimensions are not better or worse than the Earth. They are just different.

I learned that we do not choose our parents. It is highly unlikely that our parents or our brothers and sisters come from the same dimension as we do.

In my life, just prior to the time I came to Earth, I was in a dimension that was very different from Earth. I was born in a body that appeared to be semi-transparent. I could float. I was surrounded by large groups of people who were also floating. In fact, everyone was effortlessly gliding around objects that appeared like buildings. Everyone was gliding or flying. My body moved like a high speed race car at Indianapolis, except that there was no noise. And in this place I had many wonderful friends. There was more than a feeling of being close to them. I really felt in love with them. I never wanted to leave them.

I don't know how long I stayed in this place, but one day we were told that it would be necessary to travel to a new place and to have a new body. I was told that although we lived in a happy place, it was incomplete because it lacked the physical world. Here, in our world, we could feel, but only in a very subtle way. We were told in order to grow in Spirit, we would have to learn how to live in a physical world. We learned that there are many physical worlds, and although the experiences on them are similar, each one has a specific lesson to teach. The world where we were going would teach us one of our greatest lessons. We were told that it is the best place in the universe to learn how to love.

A large group of us, numbering in the thousands, were scheduled to go to this world, a place that the inhabitants called Earth. I learned that the Earth is a very special planet, because it is sort of a melting pot of souls who incarnate on it from thousands of different planets in the universe. I was told that once I incarnated on Earth, I would forget my former life, and I would not remember my friends.

During my Earth journey, I would meet friends who had come from my former dimension, and I would recognize them as kindred spirits, and because we tended to group together, we would tend to form groups together on Earth. If we met a kindred soul, we might fall in love with them all over again. We might tend to think of them as a soul mate. Actually, they are not soul mates. There really is no such thing. There are simply many souls that vibrate in wonderful ways that compliment us. These souls are like our long lost brothers and sisters. We were told to relish the times when we bumped into them on Earth, but not to forget that our primary purpose was to learn how to love in a physical body. That is why we would choose to go there.

I learned that through our lifetimes, we really do have free will. We really can choose what we want to experience. The only thing that limits our choice is our own consciousness, our own awareness. The purpose of reincarnation is simply to expand our awareness so that we can live in harmony with ourselves, with each other, and with our planet.

I learned that there is a divine purpose for the universe. Everything in the universe is on purpose. There is a purpose for the angels, for the stars, for the planets, for the Earth, for the rocks, plants, animals, and for human beings. The purpose for human beings is to discover and live their gift.

Each soul is given a special gift before coming to Earth. We are to discover our gift and then give it away to others. Not everyone discovers their gift in the first incarnation, so they come back until they find it and learn to give it away. Human beings are not to escape their humanity, but are to fully live their humanity in time and space. It is the general purpose for all human beings to bring peace to the planet Earth, through the healing power of love.

I learned we can only know our purpose in relation to the healing of our planet. We must focus and concentrate on living the fulfilled life on the planet Earth. Other purposes are not to be revealed to us until we fulfill out Earthly purposes.

I learned that on Earth we have three bodies: We have a gross material body called the physical body. We have a mental body, sometimes called the psychic body, and we have a spiritual body, sometimes called the noetic body. When a person dies on Earth, only the gross material body dies. All memory, recollections, and personality are carried in the psychic body. Death does not change our awareness. The only change that takes place is that we leave behind our gross material body.

We have an immortal soul. It is our Essence, our Divine Individuality. It is our point of conscious awareness. It is also the perceiver of our universe. Our soul also acts as the creative distributor of Universal Power. We receive this power directly from the Archangels.

It was revealed to me that we live in a spiritual Universe. It is governed by Immutable Law and is sustained by Divine Love. This love energy moves from God, particularizes itself through the Archangels, and finds its way into our soul.

Our souls are the opening to Universal Spirit. What we call our mind and our body, is simply the use that we make of Universal Energy.

Our soul tends to become what it identifies with. If it identifies with body or the material world, it becomes materialistic. If it identifies only with mind, it becomes egoistic and gets stuck in its personality. At higher levels, the soul begins to incorporate what is called 'Divine Individuality' and functions directly from its contact with the Archangels.

The soul is the executive authority of the individual. It distributes energy from the Archangels, through mind, and into body. At first it does this unconsciously and in a limited way. The more the soul opens itself to the energy of the Archangels, the more it efficiently distributes this spiritual energy.

We live in a dynamic energy system. The purpose of the universe at every moment is to actualize the soul, pouring more and more energy into it.

As I continued this experience, the message that came to me, over and over again, was that there is no death. We are immortal souls. There is that part of us that is untouched by events, that is unconditioned, that never suffers. Our soul also functions as our container of continuity. It moves us from one dimension to the next. The soul is a vehicle. When we make the transition called physical death, there is a continuity of our soul consciousness that moves onward.

These words came to me, "Coming to grips with physical death is an absolute prerequisite to living a joyful life on the Earth." The second message that continually moved through me was the message of love, that our purpose on Earth is to learn to love all sentient beings and to love the Earth. When we learn to embrace all aspects of life, (what we call good and bad including death) with wonder and compassion, we begin to understand the true meaning of love.

We are not separate from life. We are part of an interconnected whole. I then heard these words:

"You are to be subject to the authority of life, to the authority of God. Surrender to it. You are to let go and let God actively co-create in your life and the life of all humanity in the wonderful, awe-inspiring progression of life. Do not try to predict the outcome of your life, but learn to flow and participate in the process.

"Your purpose is to change your behavior from an egocentric individual to a soul-actualized individual, and therefore, change the planet. This is your revolutionary call. But it is a revolution that uses love and compassion rather than violence and manipulation. There is nothing that love cannot heal. And when you return to Earth, you will be given the ways and means to communicate this truth to others. This is your mission, this is your purpose."

As these words were spoken, I found myself back in the large hall, immediately in front of the altar. There were seven candles on the altar, and a voice said, "Light the first candle." I did not know where the light came from, but somehow, from my body at my heart area, a flame arose and lit the first candle.

In front of me a form began to appear. At first it appeared as red earth, but slowly began to take the shape of a huge man in a red robe. He towered over me. As he expanded his arms, I felt as if I were being caressed by the Earth itself.

Chapter Nine

Aneal – The Archangel of Life

"I am Aneal, Archangel of Life and Archangel of the Earth. You belong to the Earth. You are not meant to escape it, but to live here in harmony with nature. You are the custodians, caretakers, and wise, loving stewards of this beautiful planet."

"I am Aneal," he said. "I am the Archangel of Life. My essence is Life. I am the life-force of all living creatures. It is my responsibility to direct the life force from the Earth into human beings and animals. The air that you breathe is more than oxygen and chemicals. It is the energy of God that animates you. It is my energy that grounds you to the Earth. As you contemplate my life, my security, and my energy, you are connecting with your own body, other living creatures and the Earth itself. You feel a sense of balance and harmony and an inter-connection with all life. My color is red which symbolizes life from the red Earth.

"My energy does not go directly into humans. It is sent into the Earth, energizing the planet. Then, my energy is drawn out of the Earth and moves into human beings at the base of the spine. My energy vortex corresponds with your first energy center found at the base of the spine. This is the first of seven centers of energy in your body. These centers are not in your physical body but in your etheric or psychic body.

"Often, my energy is stored at the base of the spine of the individual and is not released. This is because many people are self-centered and are afraid to give this energy away. This energy is not yours. It is universal. You are simply a distributor of Divine Energy. You are to distribute this energy to your fellow humans and give it back to the planet."

"How do I open myself to your energy?" I asked.

"The first thing is to be aware of the Earth," the angel said. "You must feel the Earth, commune with it like a lover. Feel the interconnectedness of all life, the plants, the rain forests, the animals. See the Earth as a holy and sacred place. Take off your shoes and feel the grass beneath your feet. When you have the chance, go to the mountains or the sea and practice breathing in my energy by focusing your breath at the base of your spine.

"However, breathing it is not enough. You must make a conscious decision not to store my energy but circulate it. This will help open the other energy systems in your body."

"Does this mean that your energy flows up from the Earth to the bottom of my spine and then is released into higher energy centers?" I asked.

"Yes, that's right," Aneal answered. "But the centers aren't really higher in the sense of superior. They are just located higher in the body. My purpose is not only to supply you with the basic life force, but to ground you, to help you harmonize with the Earth and bring order to your life.

"In a real sense, you belong to the Earth. You are not meant to escape it, but to live there in harmony with nature. You are the custodians and caretakers of the planet. It is your purpose to watch over the delicate balance of the various systems of the Earth.

"I am also the Archangel of the Air, as well as the Archangel of the Earth. As you contemplate my order and stability, I will increase the energy in your body.

"I bring a message to your people. The message is one of ecological balance. You must tell the people that the planet is be treated with holy respect.

"The key is to see your planet as alive, as holy and sacred. Praise and give thanks to the Earth. There must be peace with the planet, with the plants, and with the animals before there can be peace among people. The first people knew this."

"You stimulate many questions," I said. "Are you saying that we should somehow go back to nature and turn our backs on our modern society?"

"No, not at all," the angel said. "You cannot force anything. You can only allow. There will be some individuals who will have a greater inclination to live more simply in nature. The key, remember, is balance and harmony. Many people need to live in the cities. They use mass transit, work in tall buildings. But it is important for all of us to take time to be outside, to commune with nature. Cities need to have gardens, parks, trees and animals."

"How are we injuring the Earth?" I asked. "Is modern Western lifestyle compatible with developing your energy?"

"You already know how you're injuring the planet, from air pollution, to the hole in the ozone, to the cutting of rain forests. But if you focus on these individual problems, you are focusing on effects. Have you noticed that when a group of people become self-righteous about anything, an equal and opposite group appears, and they are just as self-righteous. Then, suddenly, you're engaged in rhetoric, a war of words that polarizes people into positions. Very little is accomplished that way.

"Hear my message clearly. You are to turn away from effect and turn to spiritual communion.

"If you begin to teach the value that the Earth is a holy and sacred place, and that people derive life energy from the Earth, attitudes towards specific things will automatically change. Remember, every human being has this energy system within their body that communicates an innate sense of knowingness that the Earth is to be treated with love and respect. So concentrate on prayer, meditation, and opening your energy system at the base of your spine, and these problems will begin to resolve themselves."

"What would a new Earth look like if all people fully opened this base energy center?" I asked.

"That we cannot know, because human consciousness will always interact in wonderful and spontaneous ways. But we can say that pollution of our air, our rivers and streams will end. Graffiti will be unheard of. The citizens of the Earth will have a natural pride in their community," said the angel.

"That sounds utopian to me," I said.

"It's not," replied the angel. "Once you begin to operate from a spiritual base, you begin to function from cause and not effect. You begin to tap into the Love Energy of the Universe, a power that can change anything, that knows no limitation, where seeming 'miracles' become naturals."

"You have already taken the first step joining in my communion with the Earth. If you wish to call my energy forth, find a quiet place, go into meditation, focus your breathing at the base of your spine and use this invocation."

As he began to say these words his form began to dissolve back into red earth.

*"Aneal, Angel of the Air, Angel of the Earth, Essence of Life,
    breathe your life into me now.*

Make your stability and order manifest in my life today.

*May your presence and energy of the Earth
    fill me with the delight of nature.*

*May I know my connectedness with the earth,
    the seas, the rocks, the trees, the plants, the animals and
    my fellow humans.*

May your Life permeate my soul.

Aneal, Angel of the Air, Angel of the Earth, Essence of Life,

May you fill my entire being with your life energy

*I am open, I am receptive, I radiate with your Life Energy
    now."*

Chapter 10

Camael – The Archangel of Joy

"I am Camael, the Archangel of Joy. As you experience my Joy, you will realize that at your essence you are immortal and you will know nothing can harm you. Dare to be vulnerable. You are free when you become carefree."

ANGEL QUEST

And I again felt the flame move out of my heart center and light the second candle. There appeared to me an angel in an orange robe. She had long blonde hair.

She looked at me and said, "I am Camael, the Archangel of Joy. My essence is Joy. It is my responsibility to help make your life one of joy. Joy begins with passion, and passion is the beginning of enthusiasm, a zest for life. Without passion there can be no true living. My color is orange, which symbolizes the consuming fire of passion that leads to true joy.

"People in the Western world today are afraid of passion. They're afraid of becoming over emotional, of losing control. There is too much emphasis on logic and objectivity. You must understand by now, because everything is related to everything else and because everything effects everything else, there is no such thing as objectivity. An observer cannot detach himself from his observation. Yet, people continue to try. It's because they desperately want control, but control can only lead to destruction.

"Passion is especially lacking in the United States. People are much too cautious. As a result, they suppress their second energy center. If Archangels became frustrated, I would be one of the most frustrated, because more and more humans in the West are closing off their passion center. My energy vortex corresponds to your second energy system found in the pelvic area in your body. In your physical body, it manifests as sexual energy. It is not sexual energy, but it is passion."

"I don't understand," I said. "How can this center be shutting down? It seems there is more sex and violence in American society now than ever before. People are very angry and outraged."

"That's because you don't understand how this energy flows and how it works in the human body," Camael replied.

"Energy is like a river," she said. "It must flow. It must seek its positive outlet. When this second center is blocked, the energy inverts. It turns in upon itself, and manifests as rage and violence. There is a difference between the creative energy of passion and the destructive energy of rage and angry emotion. It is the same energy, but in rage it is suppressed and inverted. It's like a pressure cooker, the energy builds up and, sooner or later, the energy explodes into violent and angry reactions.

"But true passion creates feeling, where rage is negative emotion. As your passion center opens fully it turns to joy and connects and balances the other centers in your body. You intuitively know the difference between the true feeling of joy and negative emotions.

"As for sexual activity in your society, this has nothing to do with creativity, passion and joy. It is exploitive. It is the body's attempt to release negative energy. When people feel frustrated, when they think that their creativity and expression are being blocked, they engage in more sex. They use one another as objects for sexual gratification. Their bodies cry for release. They seek orgasms, but, at the same time, this physical release leaves them cold and empty.

"People know when they're being treated as sex objects. They know when they are being exploited. And the result is the second center begins to shut down even more. The inner fire and passion begins to die. The inner energy is missing, and when that happens, the anguish becomes greater. People cry out for help and try to find it in the material world of sex and drugs. I can hear their cries and feel their pain."

"What can I do?" I asked.

The angel answered, "As you become more clairsentient, you will actually be able to feel this center shutting down in people. This is especially true for large numbers of women who have been sexually molested in your society. They have shut down this center, because they were abused when they were young. Outwardly they appear normal, but inwardly they are cautious and cold. They are afraid of truly living the passionate life. They are afraid to become vulnerable, to open and expose their true feelings, because the pain is too great. The same is true of men in America, but for a different reason. They've been taught not to express their emotions. Again, they have confused feelings with ideas of weakness. To cast men in the role of strong, logical and dependable types has been a terrible injustice. We must open the second center of joy. You must be willing to become totally vulnerable, to become as a child again, to feel your genuine and spontaneous feelings that you felt when you were three years old."

"How can I become more passionate?" I asked.

"The answer is in surrender," Camael said. "Surrender to me and my energy. Dare to be vulnerable. When you realize that at your essence, you are immortal and nothing can harm you, you will understand that to fully live in life, you must be willing to take chances. You must be willing to take risks."

"But what if the pain is too great?" I said. "What if the past abuse, the scarring is too severe? What if I'm just too scared?"

"The first thing to do," answered Camael, "is to acknowledge your fear and then to bless your past. Remember, your past is what has gotten you to this place of choice. You can really never be free unless you can become carefree. That's what joy is all about. And then pray. Open your heart and mind. Pray that my passion and my joy comes into you and revitalizes you and lifts you up.

"Some of your religions in America are good at surrendering. They call it opening to the Holy Spirit, and they dance, sing, meditate, and they invoke the Spirit. And it works, because they open themselves to God or to Jesus or to Holy Spirit. My holy energy comes to them and fills them with The Light. Now it's true that they might interpret this overwhelming feeling of Spirit in different ways, many say it's the Spirit of God or the Holy Comforter, some say they are baptized with fire, some say they are living the Pentecostal experience, and still others say that Jesus has entered their hearts.

"It doesn't matter what the interpretation is. Those are human ideas about of the process. They depend upon the individual belief system. But the result is the same. My energy enters them and transforms them into passionate and enthusiastic human beings who delight in life. Hallelujah. Praise God. It gets my juices going.'

"I do have to admit," I said, "that you appear to be very animated now. Much more so than when you first appeared to me."

"Yes, Yes," Camael said. "Because my joy is real; it's the aliveness of life; it is what's important. It's what I'm in love with."

"Okay," I said. 'You got me convinced. But I've read about a lot of people who are so repressed and blocked at this second center that they don't even know it. They can't even remember the memories of their childhood, because they are too painful. How can we help them?"

"We must allow them to find their own way," she said. "For some, this may mean therapy. Forgiveness plays a key role. At some point, a shift must occur. The true purpose of any therapy is not to discover reasons why we are blocked, but it is to release the past so that we can totally and affirmatively open and surrender to God. Everyone must grow in their own way. We cannot push, but we can allow. The true and ancient meaning of psychotherapy is to nourish the soul. We must go back to that true purpose.

"As you begin to feel this passion move through you, it is the first step towards compassion for others who are still blocked, so we must also pray for them and with them."

"How can I call forth your energy?" I asked.

"During your meditation, focus your breath in your pelvic area and use this invocation," answered Camael.

As she began this chant, her body began to turn into a glowing orange flame, filling the room with a great orange light.

> *"Camael, Camael, Angel of Joy, come to me now.*
> *Fill me with your passion and enthusiasm.*
> *Let me feel at the deepest level of my being.*
> *As I merge with your energy, let me become totally alive and*
>   *intoxicated with your enthusiasm.*
> *I am alive, I am immersed in livingness.*
> *I am passionately in love with life.*
> *I open myself to the true joy of living.*
> *I am receptive to your healing energy of Joy.*
> *I unite with the energy of Life within me.*
> *My life is ordered in pure Joy.*
> *Camael, Camael, Angel of Joy,*
> *May the essence of your Joy be my Joy now."*

Be Open About Angels

"If you are open, the angels will assist you
and make their presence known,
for you have already entertained angels unaware."

Cleo

*"I am Cleo, revealing to you the
wisdom and beauty of your soul."*

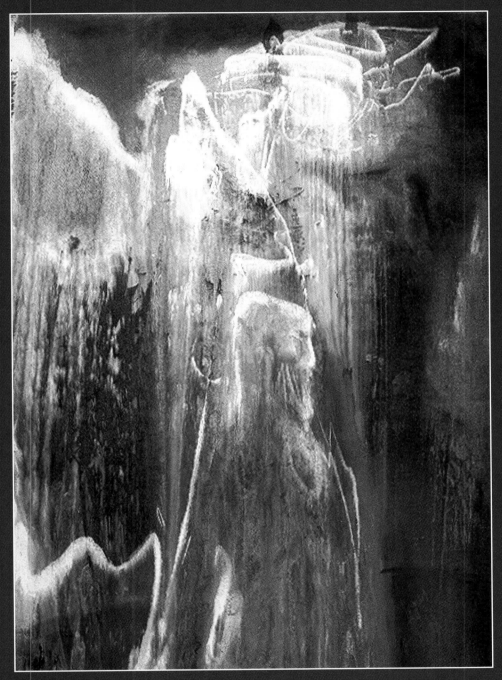

The Secrets of Lucifer

*"I am the Lightbearer. I am the light of the
morning star that illuminates the darkness."*

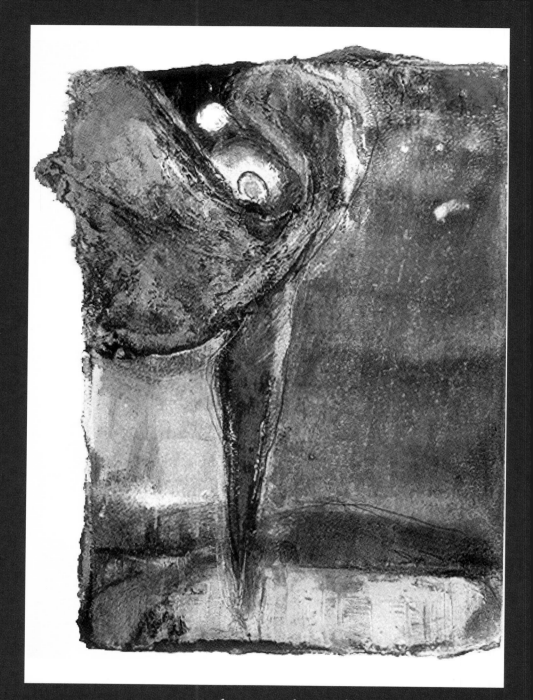

Angels & Archangels

"We greet you with profound love and light. We are here to help guide you on your journey towards wholeness. As you walk with us, know that you are loved with an everlasting love."

Camael – Archangel of Joy
"I am Camael, the Archangel of Joy. As you experience my Joy,
you will realize that at your essence you are immortal
and you will know nothing can harm you. Dare to be vulnerable.
You are free when you become carefree."

Gabriel – Archangel of Love

"I am Gabriel, the Archangel of Love. Love is a conscious decision. Make that decision, open your heart to everyone. Your heart is large enough. Remember, there is nothing that enough love cannot heal."

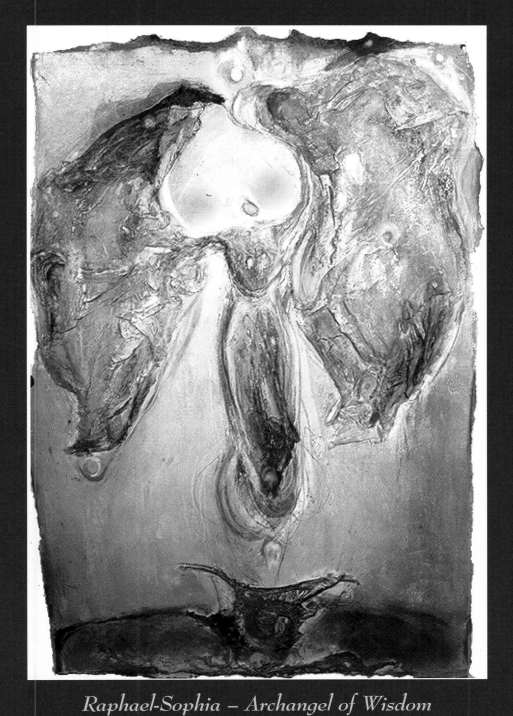

Raphael-Sophia – Archangel of Wisdom

*"I am Sophia, the Archangel of Wisdom. Love me and embrace
me and you will discover the mystical secret of wisdom.*

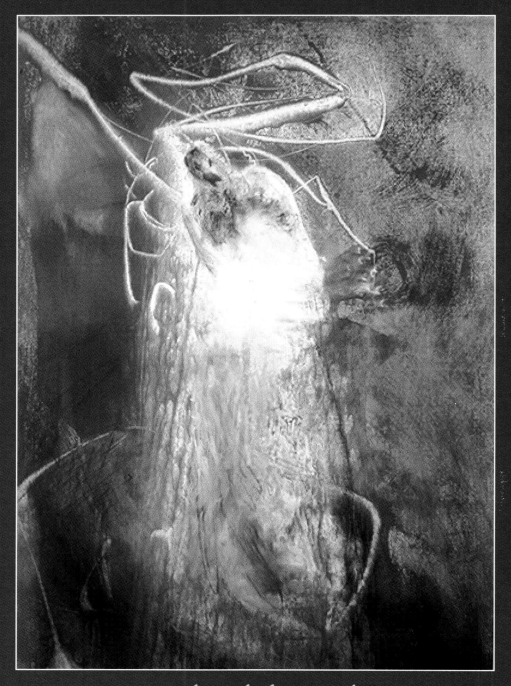

Metatron – Archangel of Spiritual Awareness
"I am Metatron, The Archangel of Light. I am the white light of
Truth, the Light of all lights. Come forward. Walk into the Light,
the Light that you cannot see but that your soul knows.
You are now ready for the last step in your journey."

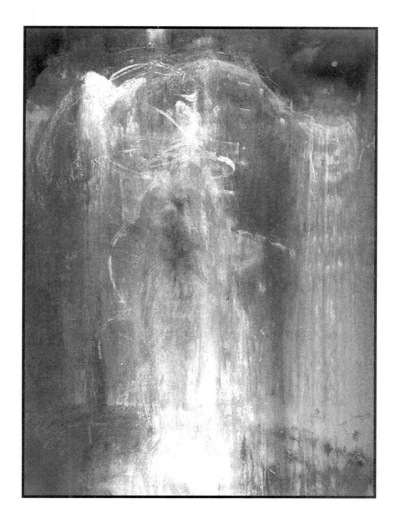

Chapter Eleven
Michael – The Archangel of Power

"I am Michael, the Archangel of Power. My gift to you is will and determination. Use my gift with love and wisdom and you will fulfill your divine destiny."

ANGEL QUEST

And as I lit the third candle, there appeared to me an angel in a yellow robe. He appeared to be very young and remarkably handsome. He gazed at me with extraordinary eyes that were all at once powerful and soft. Before me stood the most incredible being I had ever seen.

"I am Michael," he said. "I am the Archangel of Power. My essence is Power. My color is gold which symbolizes focus, determination, action, strength, courage and will. My energy vortex corresponds with the third energy system in your body. It is located in the solar plexus area, what you call the 'gut level.' It is here that the three lower energy systems come together. In your body, when your third center is open, positive and negative bioelectric forces meet. This is the place of integrated power, what you on Earth call the masculine and feminine energies. Here they meet in a polarity of quiet power."

"What do you mean by masculine and feminine energies?" I asked, "I thought there was only one energy."

'There is only one energy," Michael replied. "In its total unmanifest form before any creation, the energy is one energy in divine potential. But at the very beginning of the creative process, this energy is split into two creative forces or polarities. Without the polarity of the positive and the negative, there could be no creation.

"You humans like to anthropomorphize everything, so when you feel this energy, you give it different names. For example, the 'giving' kind of energy, you call 'masculine' and the 'receiving' kind of energy, you call 'feminine.'"

"What do you mean anthropomorphize?" I asked.

"It's just a big word that means when human beings think about things, they tend to ascribe human characteristics to what they're thinking about. The Bible says that God created humans in His image and likeness, male and female, He created them. So, the first thing people do is try to imagine God in their image. Because the Bible was written by patriarchs, people imagine God to be a male person, like some gigantic King, or something. So down through the ages, God has been depicted as some great male figure.

"When you see God as a person," Michael continued, "you are

actually separating yourself from God. God is not your father or mother, although sometimes it feels that way, 'God is Spirit, and those who worship Him, worship Him in Spirit and Truth.' Using male pronouns to describe God is unfortunate, but it's traditional. Impersonal pronouns just don't convey the same feeling. God is Spirit. He is your Divine Lover. He is much more than a father or a mother. True worship is the act of opening up to this unconditional love of God, and then giving this unconditional love back to the universe.

"For creation to occur, you need both masculine and feminine energy. Men and women on Earth have both kinds of energy. But at your state of evolution, people are not yet androgynous or fully balanced. So, what you call physical sex is necessary for procreation."

"What do you mean, not androgynous yet?" I asked.

"All creation is the result of the combination of masculine and feminine energy in flux," Michael said. "Physical creation is the result of this flux of spiritual energy. Human beings are dynamic energy systems that have a tendency to be either male shaded or female shaded. Therefore, a person will manifest physically according to his or her dominant energy bias.

"Human consciousness is constantly changing. When a state of dynamic equilibrium is obtained, people will manifest bodies that are no longer male or female oriented. They will be neither and both."

"It's hard for me to conceive of that," I said. "And I rather enjoy the difference the way it is."

"I wouldn't really worry about it," Michael said. "In Earth time, it will be thousands of years before these kinds of changes begin to occur. Many other things will have happened by then, including what is known as "conscious immortality." At that stage of development, the individual soul will actually be able to choose how he or she wishes to appear.

"But I don't know how we got into a discussion of these things. I'm here to help you open your third energy system through concentrating on my Power."

"Just one thing," I said, "before we leave the subject. There is a big concern on Earth about homosexuality, and whether or not people have choice in the matter. Is it caused by genetics or environmental factors?"

"They're asking the wrong question," Michael said. "When you ask questions from a particular view point, you invariably get wrong answers. Don't you see that you asked a closed question, using very limited terms like genetics and environment? Creation doesn't work that way. Human beings are energy systems within energy systems.

"The Universal Field of Divine Love and Intelligence creates the form of the human energy systems. Then the form itself acts upon the Field. Everything in the universe is in constant flux. All living energy systems require a continual flow of energy to maintain a dynamic stability and to grow. As I've told you, this energy is polarized into positive and negative kinds.

"The physical body that the human being manifests on Earth is a result of a particular kind of energy existing at conception. But the physical body does not determine how the human will receive and blend energy after conception. That determination is continually being made by the choice of the soul. Sexual orientation is a result of choice. Often, it is choice at an unconscious level. It is not the simple process of a one-time decision. It is a continuing and dynamic process. When you put labels on people, you're going to be wrong. People aren't like a can of beans. They change at every moment. So, these kinds of arguments that you humans use are just not realistic, because you create rigid solutions by asking the wrong questions.

"By the way, you have the same limited and rigid debate when you discuss what you call your 'abortion question.' When does life begin, at conception or when the fetus is viable?

"You don't get it. Life doesn't begin. The soul is immortal. It lives forever. You can't kill the soul. So the question doesn't make any sense. Remember, the universe is in a constant state of continual flux. Souls make choices, people make choices. The soul that decides to incarnate doesn't know if the mother will decide to end her pregnancy or not, but if she does, no harm comes to the soul. It just picks another means of incarnation. There is an infinite number of souls in an infinite number of bodies. Life on Earth has the meaning that you choose to give it. But I suppose if you didn't have these issues to talk about, then you would have to focus on more important things like transformation."

"It sounds like you're trivializing some of the important issues of our day," I said.

Michael looked at me with that same expression of compassion and unconditional love that I had felt with Cleo.

"I didn't mean to give that impression," Michael said. "That's what the third power center is all about, focus and intention. It's up to you to decide how important something is. All I'm suggesting is that before you jump into any issue with both feet, take a look at the perspective, the view point. Is there another creative and more harmonious way of looking at what you call a serious problem? What is the loving thing to do?

"Is it loving to become angry and throw people out of your heart, to call them names and separate them from you because of your own fears? You are an immortal soul, a Divine Essence. You have never been created and you can never be destroyed. You have chosen to live and operate in a particular field of energy. Fields of energy are like paradigms. They are created by focused intention, thought patterns and mental equivalents. You actually live inside of an idea. The idea determines your understanding of the meaning within your particular field. What you are doing right now, with me, by this experience, is expanding your idea of what your field is like. It's exciting, but it's unsettling. By opening yourself up to greater energy, the old paradigm ultimately cannot stand. It will change. Didn't Jesus say something about putting new wine into old wine skins?"

"How do I open myself to your power?" I asked.

"You're already doing it," answered Michael, "just by being receptive. The life energy and the joy from the two lower centers are specifically focused in the third center. It is here that you formulate a vision, a plan, and put it into action. And when you fully open to my center, you will fully develop your will and determination.

"This is the first step in conscious co-creation. It is not enough to open the three lower centers. It's necessary to choose with love and wisdom. For this, you must take my energy and move it upward into the higher centers.

"But without my will and determination and without the lower centers, you will not be grounded. You may float on a sea of love, but you will be rutterless. My center gives you decisiveness, assertiveness, qualities that are absolutely necessary for the development for Divine Individuality.

"There may be times in your life when you are indecisive, when you need to activate your determination and will, and, therefore, you can call me forth with this invocation."

And as he began to chant, Michael seemed to grow and glow, into a luminous golden flame filling my entire consciousness with his power.

'Michael, Angel of Power, come to me now
    and fill me with your clarity and decisiveness
Let me feel your presence so that I may
    act from a clear space of right action.
Allow me to blend your energies into a harmonious whole
Allow me to focus my quiet power ,
    to act decisively from strength but also from great love,
Give me courage, will and determination.
Let me consciously and creatively direct your power,
    focused in love and goodwill
    with the highest and purest intention possible.
I am open and receptive to your Power now
And I bring together my energies of Life and Joy
    and merge them into your Power.
Michael, Angel of Power,
May your essence of Power be my Power now."

ANGEL QUEST

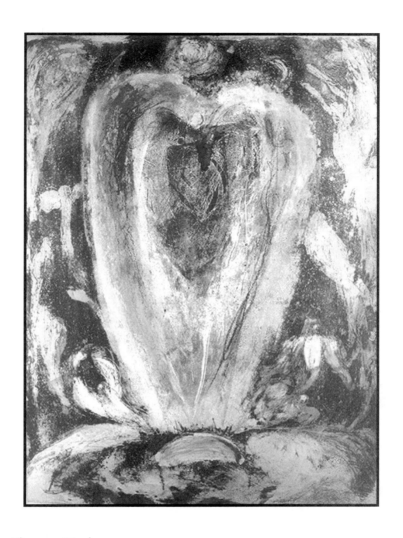

Chapter Twelve
Gabriel – The Archangel of Love

"I am Gabriel, the Archangel of Love. Love is a conscious decision. Make that decision, open your heart to everyone. Your heart is large enough. Remember, there is nothing that enough love cannot heal. "

And I turned and lit the fourth candle. There appeared to me a very beautiful angel, with long, flowing red hair and an emerald green robe, holding a lily in her hand.

"I am Gabriel," she said. "I am the Archangel of Love. My essence is Love. My color is green which symbolizes the blossoming and the fruition of love. I comfort people by sending them the energy of love. I correspond to the energy system in your body called the heart center. This is the center in your body that must be fully open in order to integrate the energy of the Earth from the lower centers and the energy of Heaven from the higher centers.

"I am the merging and the blending Archangel, the central vortex that receives all of the different energies. Without my love fully opened, it is not possible to be fully human. A person may be in touch with Earth energy, he can have his passion and emotional center open, he can be focused with will and determination from his power center, but without love, he is nothing.

"There is a great misunderstanding about my love. It is not passion or emotion. It is not that romantic feeling of falling in love. It is true unconditional givingness, with total kindness and acceptance, without expecting anything in return.

"The best description of my love comes from your own Bible in the New Testament, where it says,

> 'Love is always patient and kind. Love is never jealous.
> Love is not boastful or conceited. It is never rude and never
> seeks its own advantage. It does not take offense or store up
> grievances. Love does not rejoice at wrong doing,
> but finds its way in the truth. It is always ready
> to make allowances, to trust, to hope,
> and to endure whatever comes.'

"Pretty good stuff, huh? I helped Paul write that."

"You angels always take me back," I said. "First, I thought you were a male angel. You know, 'Gabriel blew his horn.' And, second, what do you mean you helped Paul write that?"

"Okay," Gabriel said. "You already know that we appear to you according to your dominant mode of perception and that the perceiver helps create the perception. You see me as female, because you think of love as a feminine quality, something that is received. In the Old Testament times, when the Bible was being written, I was seen in patriarchal terms. As for the horn, it's a trumpet, heralding in the age of Love on Earth. The Earth was created for one main purpose, to teach people how to love. That's why you incarnated there and why everyone comes there.

"Now, about Paul. Have you ever read his stuff?" Gabriel asked.

"I've read some of his letters," I answered. "But I haven't systematically studied him."

"Paul," said Gabriel, "was a very interesting personality. There were times when he really got in touch with his heart center and wrote some of the most beautiful and lovely things in the Bible. That's when I inspired him. Just listen to this:

> 'In the abundance of His glory,
> may God, through His Spirit,
> enable you to grow firm in power,
> with regard to your inner self,
> so that Christ may live in your hearts through faith,
> and, then, planted in love and built on love
> with all God's holy people,
> you will have the strength to grasp
> the breadth and the length, the height and the depth,
> so that knowing the love of Christ,
> which is beyond knowledge,
> you may be filled with the utter fullness of God.'

"It gives me goosebumps," Gabriel said. "That was Paul at his best. Unfortunately he also wrote when his overbearing and moralistic rigid personality got in the way. He could be self-righteous, intolerant, dogmatic, and inflexible. And when he was in that frame of mind, it was very difficult for me to break through to him.

"Anyway, I didn't appear before you to talk about Paul, or how to study the Bible. I came to tell you about love. There are two aspects of true love; the giving and the receiving. Let's talk about receiving first. Like the scripture says, love means opening your heart wide and taking in, accepting everyone right where they are without judgment, being there for others, listening, feeling as others feel, allowing yourself to be totally vulnerable, always ready to trust, to hope and endure whatever comes. This aspect of love means surrendering to God, with total faith that God knows what He is doing, that there is a Divine will and purpose behind every event and that in the long run there is nothing but good going on."

"Does it mean I have to love people I don't like?" I asked. "Do I have to love everyone?"

"It means," said the angel, "that in this aspect of love, the receiving aspect, you open your heart to everyone. Your heart is large enough. But, remember, I said there were two aspects of love. In terms of giving, you are actually sending energy to others. You are a beacon of this love energy. And when all of your energy systems are fully open, energy rushes to your heart and then you simply direct this energy from your heart to others. But, you choose to whom and how you send this love energy.

"So, my purpose is to teach you how to unconditionally accept others, and then how to focus and send your love to others. From your heart center, you are most like an angel, because you are accepting God's Love Energy, reprocessing it according to your own unique individuality, and co-creating with it, directing it outward with warmth and genuine kindness to others."

"What do you mean the Earth was created for the purpose of love?" I asked.

"People of the Earth will not be able to advance in consciousness until they have embodied my love. It's like you are stuck on the Earth until you get it. The purpose of life on Earth is not to live comfortably, or to accumulate money, or to industrialize the planet. The purpose is to love. Everything else is secondary. Remember, you learn courage by opening your power center. Now take that courage and transmute it into vulnerability and deliberately open yourself to others. Welcome them. Learn that the key to the expanding of consciousness is a conscious process, a conscious choosing to love. Love is a conscious decision. You will learn to allow the Heaven energy centers of Light, Wisdom and Beauty to come into your heart center from above. You will allow the Earth energy centers of Life, Joy and Power to flow up to your heart center from below. You must circulate all this energy in you and give it away in your own special way. You must give yourself to love. Only then will you become aware of the truth of your being.

"If you feel low or down, just know you can invoke my presence and ask me to come to you and open your heart. And I will come."

And then I saw Gabriel begin to dissolve into an emerald green energy, almost like a haze or smoke. And I began to breathe in this energy, and my whole body became full of her Divine Love.

And then Gabriel began to chant. As she chanted, I began to feel a powerful energy move in and through me. It was like my heart was expanding, getting bigger and bigger, as if I were going to burst open. It just kept growing larger and larger. I felt such a gratitude for the whole universe, from the tiniest blade of grass to the largest star.

"Gabriel, Gabriel, Angel of Love,
I call on you to open my heart.
Allow me to experience total kindness and caring.
Make my heart full of joy
so that I may comfort and nurture others.
Let my love touch others
and help with the healing process of the world,
so that each of us feels a sense of unity and wholeness.
I know there is nothing that enough love cannot heal. '
Gabriel, Gabriel, Angel of Love,
I am open , I am receptive, I am ready to give of my Love.
May your essence of Love be my Love now."

Chapter Thirteen

Uriel – The Archangel of Beauty

"I am Uriel, the Archangel of Beauty. You have the opportunity to create the free and beautiful life through the power of your conscious choice. Liberation is not escape. It is living the fulfilled life on Earth. Enlightenment doesn't mean merging your soul into a cosmic ocean. It means the that the cosmic ocean merges itself into you."

ANGEL QUEST

And I turned and lit the fifth candle. I saw the color of electric blue vibrating in front of me, and I heard a sound, a sound of harmonizing notes, with a beautiful background of heavenly meditative music. From out of the color and the sound, came a deep base voice:

"I am Uriel, the Archangel of Beauty. My essence is Beauty. My color is blue which symbolizes harmony, the formation of the creative word and the sound of communication. I am also the Archangel of music. I correspond to the center of creativity in your throat area. This is the creative center that accepts the ideas from the head and puts them into action. In the beginning was the Word. I am the Aum of the universe. It is my energy that begins the creative process. Although the very first manifestation of God is light, the universal sound is what vibrates energy into the first form. In fact, the energy vortex of each Archangel is sustained by my sound, and each Archangel has a sound that corresponds to musical notes. You are actually hearing my primary note and all of its harmonic combinations. My sound also helps activate the sounds of the other energy centers, much like a tuning fork starts other tuning forks vibrating.

"You've been told that you have seven energy centers in your 'psycho-noetic body'. Universal energy, in an undifferentiated state, flows up into your body from the Earth and up the first three energy centers into the fourth center, the heart center. But energy also flows down from what is called your crown center, through your third eye center in the middle of your forehead, and begins to vibrate as sound through my center before moving down into the heart."

"Why can't I see your form?" I asked. "All I can see is a blue flame and hear these beautiful sounds."

"You cannot see me," answered Uriel, "because I am still in the process of becoming form. I am coming into manifestation. My sound is the sound of creation coming into being.

"Let me explain to you how this creative process works. In the beginning, we all come from God and we will all return to God. But who is God? 'Who' is not the right question. Because God is not a who. It's probably better to say that God is that transcendent Reality, the Unified Field of Intelligent Energy. This Ultimate Energy is intelligent because It is on purpose, It creates everything out of Itself through some inner action upon Itself. This inner action is the ultimate mystery. Even the Archangels don't know how it works. The best approximation for a human being is that it is Divine Mystery. It is something completely and permanently beyond human understanding.

"You see, everything is energy. What you call matter is just energy in form. This form is kept in place by intention and focused attention. The Archangels, the angels, the physical universe, and all of the entities in the universe are produced by the intention and the focused attention of God.

"But this focused attention is not just outside the form penetrating in; It's inside the form penetrating out. The intelligence in this energy doesn't just come from somewhere; It comes from everywhere all at the same time. It is not static. It is dynamic.

"Now there are different points of view in this creative process. You are seeing it, hearing it, touching it, feeling it, and breathing it from a particular point of view. You are a self-conscious individualized expression of the entire process.

"But you do have within you the capacity to see this process from a different point of view. Your point of view is actually a defining experience of who you are, or, rather, who you think you are. Let's just say that whoever you think you are, you are more than that. 'I am the Person that Thou art, and Thou art the Person that I am.' Do you get it?"

"I heard that statement once before. I can't say I understand it, but I'm beginning to feel what it means," I replied.

"That's good," Uriel said. "That's better than getting it. Don't you see what's happening? You feel the Truth before you get it. Getting it is understanding it. Understanding it is the first step towards application. We confuse understanding and application with real Truth. Understanding and application are only approximations of the Truth. When you really feel it, you are the Truth.

"But the way things work is that you get to use this creative process yourself before you feel it, before you get it, and before you understand it. As soon as you become aware of yourself, you start using this creative process unconsciously. As soon as you start forming words, as soon as you begin to focus your attention, you begin to use this very process and my center begins to open in you. How effectively you use this creative process depends on how well you open up all of your other centers and how effectively you integrate these energies."

"Are you trying to tell me that I have something to do with the creation of my own experience by the use of my own creative expression?" I asked.

"Exactly," Uriel said. "You are like a film projector. Your beliefs that are stored in your mind act like a filmstrip that flows through your projector. You project selected and focused ideas outside of yourself on a screen that you call your life. Then, you perceive what you've already projected and call it reality."

"I create my own reality through my own projection?"

"Well, it's a little more complicated than that," Uriel said. "It's probably more correct to say that you participate in the creation of your own reality, because you are not the only intelligence that is projecting ideas onto your screen. Others are doing it, too. Your projector is not the only one turned on. There are billions of them focusing on the screen of life, all at the same time."

"That sounds confusing," I said. "How do I decide what I see?"

"Exactly." said the Archangel. "You decide by choosing or filtering what it is that you want to see. You get to select how you view your reality by picking a particular mosaic of the combination of all of the projections."

"How in the world do I go about doing that? There must be thousands of different combinations every second of how I could see the world."

"There are, and you do it by having a built in 'meaning selector.' You have built within you an innate desire for meaning. So you select those things that are meaningful to you and you forget about the rest."

"So that means," I said, "that each person on the Earth is projecting a particular reality and then is perceiving a particular reality, and that each reality is different?"

"Every reality is different. But many are similar. So similar, in fact, that most people think they are seeing the same thing. There are common grounds or reference points. For example, when you go into a restaurant and the waitress serves you lemon pie, and you and your friend bite into that wonderful tart and sweet taste, you're both going to taste lemon pie. But it won't taste exactly the same. The molecules of energy that are projected as the pie will be perceived slightly differently, because every individual has a unique perception."

"Okay," I said. "I think I understand the analogy of the projector. I'm both the projector and the perceiver at the same time. My light within me shines out and illuminates the filmstrip in my mind, which projects onto the screen that I think is external reality. Then I look at what I've projected and what others have projected. Then I interpret what I see so it has meaning for me, then I say that's the way it is. Okay. I get it. But where does this filmstrip come from? Do I make it?"

"This is the hard part," said Uriel. "It's like a loop. Have you ever heard of someone being in the loop or out of the loop? When you get to the 'built in meaning selector' part of the process, whereby you choose to see what it is you will see, that very act of choice creates the filmstrip that is being projected. So in one sense, what you are perceiving, determines what you will subsequently project. You are a closed system. You get back what you put out. And what you get back determines what you put out again. It's like your own paradigm, your own way of seeing things.

"So, in a way, you go through life as a mechanical man, asleep to your true nature. Perception creates projection, which creates perception, which creates projection, same old, same old, ad nauseam."

"If that's true, it's very boring," I said.

"Yes," the Archangel said. "For most people it is very boring. It's like having a library of five hundred films that you continually watch over and over again and call it your life. You know the expression

'Get a life?' It means, 'stop doing the same things over and over again, expecting different results."

"Can we get out of the loop? Can we become less mechanical?"

"Sure," Uriel said. "The easiest thing to do is to expand your film library. You do this by opening your mind and allowing yourself to see more of others' projections. You learn to discriminate, to step outside of your own creations and expand the loop. You learn the art of detachment. While this will give you more variety, it will not address the fundamental question. Somehow you have to actually get outside the loop, not just expand it, but to step out of it, to transcend it, to see it from a different dimension."

"Wow. How can I do that?"

"There is only one way," the Archangel replied. "You have to be willing to open yourself to an energy source that is greater than anything you can presently conceive of. You have to surrender to something greater than your own filmstrip or the filmstrip of any other person who is projecting. You have to let go. In simple terms, it means real worship. It means asking or invoking a Higher and Greater Energy Source to permeate you with Its power. It means to truly love God. This is the only way to transcend the loop. And you can't do it second hand, through someone else's theology.

"There are people on the Earth who can point the way to the Truth, but you have to find It yourself. If you ask that your energy systems be open to receive newer and greater energy, if you open your heart to the Presence of God, and if you continually pray, you will be given expanded energy.

"Do you remember the saying, 'It shall be done unto you according to your belief?' Well, that statement is true. But, with it, you will stay in the loop that you have created.

"The subtle distinction is that Jesus said, 'Be it done unto you according to your faith.' This means a willingness to leave your belief systems behind and reach beyond anything that you have ever known, to take the leap of faith and pray that this new energy comes to you, and worship God, not the God of tradition, but the God of Ultimate Reality, the God of Ultimate Mystery. And, then, as Emerson said,

'May God fire your soul.'"

"Can you tell me more about reincarnation," I asked. "Is there reincarnation?"

"That depends on what you understand reincarnation to be. You already know that the soul or your spiritual body is immortal. After what you call death on Earth, the soul does continue to express. Desire for expression, for creation, is built into the very fabric of the universe. The soul wishes to express and that desire is also eternal. Therefore, it is inevitable that the soul will take on some form or vehicle of expression. But the universe contains many dimensions. There are an infinite variety of expressions on other planes."

"Does the soul ever choose to come back to Earth?' I asked.

"Sometimes it does. The soul has free choice and can choose to incarnate anywhere. These dimensions I'm telling you about are not in a hierarchy or like a school. You don't have to fully live in one dimension in order to experience another. A soul may return to Earth to be with loved ones, to search for a lost love, or simply because it experienced a good time the last time around."

"What about karma?" I asked.

"Most Westerners are influenced by either the Hindu or Buddhist concept of reincarnation and karma. Hinduism thinks of reincarnation as misery and a sorrowful burden, a bondage from which to escape. Buddhism talks about liberation from rebirth. Both philosophies teach that people incarnate because of karma or earthly cravings. These spiritual philosophies were formulated when there was great suffering on the Earth, when, for ordinary people in India, to live was to suffer. So, these philosophies must be understood in that context.

"Implicit in their philosophies is the futility of making things better on Earth, because a soul's duty is not to live in joy on Earth, but to escape the Earth, to be liberated from it. But one of your purposes in coming to the Earth is to make the planet better. Jesus was right when he said, 'You are to be in the world but not of it.' Enlightenment doesn't mean merging your soul into a cosmic ocean. It means that the cosmic ocean merges itself into you. And that is very different. Liberation is not escape. It is living the fulfilled life on Earth."

"So, what about karma?" I asked.

"Karma is not a force that keeps you tied to the Earth. It is a law that helps free you as an individual. Karma in Hinduism and Buddhism is the belief that your actions in this lifetime determine what happens to you in another lifetime.

"In Christianity it states, 'You reap what you sow.' And this is true. There is a universal law that says you get back what you give out. So, instead of karma, we might call it karmic tendencies based on the accumulated knowledge of the soul. Through lifetimes of incarnations, the soul has accumulated knowledge, so it has a stored bank of knowledge upon which it makes choices in this lifetime. But knowledge is not the same as wisdom. It is simply the belief systems that the soul has accepted. You experience life according to your belief systems. You will see the world according to the way you project your beliefs into it. People never react to what is actually happening. They react according to their beliefs."

"Wait a minute," I said. "The starving child in Africa is not projecting poverty. The deformed child is not projecting the fact that he has no legs."

"Projection is not limited to the belief of the individual," the Archangel said. "It is a product of race belief. Human beings create their own reality by their own thought. If the consciousness of the race thinks poverty, then that is the result. If the consciousness of the race thinks deformity, then that is the result."

"I can't buy this explanation," I said.

"Then that is the result," said the angel. "You can accept only at the level of your conscious embodiment. Just keep an open mind and more and more will become clear to you. The goodness of the universe will bring you home. Trust.

"There is always a relationship between the universal and the individual. It is not a duality. It is a unity of communion. God has provided all the ingredients for a happy and joyful life wherever you decide to incarnate. But, it's up to you to decide what you will do with these ingredients."

"I still have questions about why babies are born deformed, why children die of terrible diseases, and why so many people have to suffer," I said.

"And the answers to all these questions are the same," said the Archangel. "The soul does not suffer. There is that aspect of you that watches all the experiences, but is not touched by sickness, disease, or death. Remember, you are a being in a dimension of time and space, where everyone is free to choose how to experience life. As a soul, you may choose to be born into a family. The family may choose to do things that hurt you. Your soul is not omniscient in the sense that you know what is going to happen to you in the future. You can't predict what other people may choose to do. Many different choices may impact your life. It's called spontaneity and going with the flow.

"A father with self-destructive tendencies may affect the life of his son. A mother who is an alcoholic may affect the life of her daughter. We cannot predict in advance how these things will occur. We can train ourselves to be open, to listen, and to choose what we think at the time will be for the highest good of all. We all have the capacity to do that. Just remember, any tendency can be overcome with enough love. Love changes everything."

"Sometimes," I said, "I have trouble understanding the difference between judgment and choice. When I make choices, when I prefer to do one thing rather than another, am I judging? When I prefer to be with one person rather than another, am I judging?"

"No," said the Archangel. "As you become more and more enlightened, you will not judge any one for any reason any time. Do you get it? Do you understand the difference between judgment and choice?

"You are here in time and space to choose, to exercise your dominion, to take responsibility for yourself. That does not include judgment."

"But what about people who hurt you, or people who hurt society?"

I asked.

"Don't buy into their stuff. Choose. Don't judge."

"How do I know what to choose? If we really are all intercon-nected, won't my choices affect other people?"

"Yes. Every choice you make affects others. That is why you must choose at the highest level of your consciousness, at the deepest level of your understanding. The more you learn, the more you open your-self up to wisdom. The more you open yourself up to wisdom, the more responsibility you have. Choose wisely, but choose for your highest and best good. And if you do, it will be for the highest and best good for all.

"I know that philosophers in your world are fond of pointing out moral dilemmas or arguing that each choice adversely affects some-one else. But your job is to align yourself with your spiritual aware-ness to the best of your ability, to allow wisdom to come through you, to articulate your choice, and then to act. It is possible, in a differ-ent situation, if you had been more aware, you would have made a different choice. But that's not life or the spontaneity of living. You must choose on the basis of your deepest understanding and choose now."

As, Uriel said this, the flame of electric blue grew larger and larg-er and began to envelop me. But, for some reason, I was not afraid, and I willingly allowed myself to become consumed by the blue flame. I did not feel any sensation of heat or burning, but, rather, it was a purification. I was being immersed in the essence of the uni-verse. And I heard these words come to me:

"Uriel, Uriel, Angel of Beauty,
may your creative energy flow to me,
a new energy, an energy greater than my previous
ability to comprehend or believe.
As I open myself to you, I open myself
to the creative sound of the Universe.
Your musical energy flows through my soul and I hum inside.

I open to new dimensions in Spirit.
My old ways of thinking are changed and transcended,
and I see the world as bright, shining and beautiful.
And I hear the Word of God singing,
'Behold I make all things new.'
'Uriel, Uriel, Angel of Beauty,
May your essence of Beauty be my Beauty now."

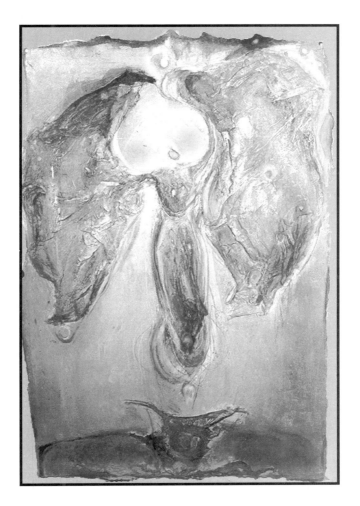

Chapter Fourteen

Raphael - Sophia
The Archangel of Wisdom

"I am Sophia, the Archangel of Wisdom. Love me and embrace me and you will discover the mystical secret of Wisdom. Wisdom is brilliant. She never fades. The radiance of Wisdom is overwhelming, beyond ordinary light. Wisdom is the light of lights."

Then I lit the sixth candle, and the room became brighter than the sun. I immediately became blinded. I could not see.

"Close your eyes," I heard a voice say. "You are not accustomed to such an intense light. But do not fear, for I will heal you." And I felt fingers moving over my eyelids. It felt like moisture being applied.

"Now, open your eyes slowly," the voice said, "very slowly." And as I looked, I saw before me what can only be described as 'The Shining One'. He, or was it she, was shining all over. Her face was aglow with light and a lavender light surrounded her body.

The body, although covered with a semi-transparent robe was beautifully sculptured. The hair was long and dark, and the skin seemed to radiate a light blue-red energy. The way the robe was wrapped, it was impossible to determine whether this gorgeous being was male or female.

"Hold my hand," he/she said, "and I will very slowly acclimate you to my energy. I am vibrating at a very low frequency so that you can tolerate my presence. It can be very dangerous for humans to gaze upon me unless they're fully prepared, because the light energy is so great."

When this being took my hand, it was almost impossible to describe the feeling. It was like a current that was moving through my body. For the first time, I noticed my own form. I had the same body that I had back on Earth, but it appeared, as I perused myself, to be a much younger and much more slender body. I appeared to be a young man of about twenty-six. And as I watched my body, it began to glow, although not nearly as bright as this angelic form.

"You are confused," the voice said. 'The reason you cannot tell if I am masculine or feminine is because I am both. I have two names. In the Christian Bible I appear as male and am known as Raphael. My name means 'The Shining One Who Heals.' I am the power of healing, and I can regenerate or heal any physical body. I have come to tell you the secrets of healing, of total health, and of transmutation of the human body at the cellular level. You have already noticed that as you receive my energy, your body appears younger and very healthy and vibrant.

"I am Raphael, the Archangel of the Sun, the Archangel of Healing. But my name is also Sophia, the Archangel of Wisdom. My essence is Wisdom. My color is majestic purple that symbolizes peace. Peace comes to the one who embraces true Wisdom, who seeks total healing. Jesus said, 'Peace I give unto you, not as the world gives, do I give unto you._

"In my nature as Sophia, I appear as feminine to those who have seen me. But in essence I am the shining light emanating both wisdom and healing, both masculine and feminine. I am what you are to become."

"Why do you have two names?" I asked.

"It's simply an anomaly of human history," she answered. "Remember, the Bible was written by men, and when they sensed my presence, whether it was with Abraham or Tobias, I was seen as a male angel. And because of my healing presence, I was called Raphael, 'The Shining One Who Heals.' But I also appeared to Solomon when he prayed to God for Wisdom.

"Solomon saw me and felt me as Sophia, the Feminine Presence of Wisdom. Solomon wrote about me in great detail in a biblical book called *The Book of Wisdom*. But the early church fathers were very much afraid of feminine energy, and they not only excluded the book from the Bible, but blasphemed my energy."

"What do you mean blasphemed?" I said.

"I am the energy of Divine Mother. Before there was any creation, I was present with the Master Craftsman, ever at play in His presence, helping to create all other energy systems, giving birth to the universe.

"Because Western civilization came from a patriarchal bias there was a great fear of the feminine goddess, the feminine principle. My energy and power were denied in the West. There were even attempts to degrade me in your literature, seeing me as a temptress, a whore, or a fallen angel. A careful study of Western religion will reveal the schizophrenic view of the early church scholars. On one hand, they recognized the profound insight of Solomon in courting my feminine side. On the other hand, they felt very threatened by my intuitive wisdom that their rational intellect could not understand.

"This dynamic tension is quite complex. It has existed in the Christian church from the beginning. It also exists in your society and in your male-female relationships. The key to healing is to honor and embrace the feminine in your culture, civilization, and in your spirituality. Allow yourself to court my feminine energy and be immersed in my loving presence."

"How do I court your energy?" I asked. I was amazed that she continued to hold my hand and that my body was getting brighter and brighter.

"I am going to tell you how," she answered. "First, do not concern yourself with the masculine side. That is already overdeveloped on the Earth. Understand how I have appeared in your spiritual traditions. Solomon gives a lot of information about me, and it is found in the Book of Proverbs and in the Book of Wisdom.

"In the beginning, before there was any creation, I was with what you call God. I was also with the Divine Logos, the Archangel Metatron, the Archangel of the Crown. I know this is difficult to understand because what I am telling you is part of the divine mystery of creation. But, in the beginning, before there was creation, there was only God, God unmanifest, God in the form of all potentiality, and, at the same time, God, the no form, God of no potentiality.

"Then, the first act of creation occurred. The first act of creation was the emanation from God of the Masculine Principle, symbolized by the energy vortex of Metatron, the Archangel of the Crown, and the creation of the Feminine Principle, Sophia, the Archangel of Wisdom.

"Do you remember in the Bible, in the *Book of John*, It says, 'In the beginning was the Word. The Word was with God. The Word was God in the beginning.' That scripture is a mystical key to unveiling the mystery of creation, but it must be combined with the scripture from Proverbs, which states:

> *"From everlasting, I was firmly set.*
> *From the beginning, before the Earth came into being,*
> *before the mountains were settled, before the hills,*
> *I came to birth. When He fixed the Heavens, I was there.*
> *When He traced the foundations of the Earth,*
> *I was beside the Master Craftsman,*
> *delighting Him day by day, ever at play in His presence,*
> *at play everywhere on His Earth,*
> *delighting to be with the children of men."*

"Yes," said Sophia. "This is the answer. Logos is Metatron, the Archangel of Light in the masculine. Sophia is the same creative Principle in the feminine. And when the two come together, the Christ is born.

"The Christ, The Anointed One, is not merely Logos, The Masculine Principle of Metatron, but is the perfect progeny of Logos and Sophia.

"The Christ was not born in human history of time and space. The Christ is eternal. The Christ is the prototype of what a human can become and is the offspring of eternal masculine and feminine spiritual vortices. The Christ is the prototype created out of my energy and the energy of Metatron, Sophia and Logos."

"I thought Jesus and Christ were one and the same," I said .
"They are and they are not," Sophia responded. "The human that you call Jesus lived at a particular time. But, at the same time, he was totally identified with the mystical Christ. He was the example of what every human can become. He fully opened all seven of his energy centers. He became the Essence of Life, Joy, Power, Love, Beauty, Wisdom, and Light.

"Human civilization took a wrong turn when the patriarchal church tried to kill and degrade feminine energy. Jesus came in the form of a man, but actually was a complete blend of the masculine and the feminine, of Heaven and Earth. And now is the time to bring the truth back to the people, the truth of Jesus, the truth of the Christ, and the truth of the angels.

"You have, in your 'psycho-noetic body', an energy system found in the middle of your forehead, called your 'third eye center'. This center corresponds to the pineal gland in the physical body, the pineal gland, which, by the way, has atrophied, because the feminine principle has atrophied on Earth.

"That is why you became blinded when I first appeared to you. Your body was not used to my energy. The reason that healing is now taking place in you is because your third eye center is opening up to my love and my power. I am the Archangel of Wisdom, the Angel of the Third Eye.

"Solomon knew this when he wrote, 'Wisdom is brilliant. She never fades. The radiance of Wisdom is overwhelming, beyond ordinary light, Wisdom is the light of lights. By those who love her, she is readily seen. By those who seek her, she is readily found. She anticipates those who desire her by making herself first known.'"

"You said you came to teach me the secrets of healing," I said.

"Yes," said Sophia. "The secret is quite simple. You are meant to have all of your energy systems completely open, just as the Master Jesus did. The deliberate act of suppressing feminine energy has gone on too long, and, as a result, sickness has come to humanity. Health means harmony and balance. It means an unblocked flow and harmonizing of both masculine and feminine energies in the human body. Until this is done, there cannot be total health."

"But women on Earth become ill the same as men. Don't they have more of your energy?" I asked.

"Neither sex has much of my energy. Women may have more than men, but it is just as imbalanced. Real health means a much greater flow of all of the energy systems. Again, the secret has already been revealed in the *Book of Wisdom*. The coming of Wisdom begins with the sincere desire for instruction. 'Eagerness for instruction means loving her. Loving her means keeping her laws. Attention to her laws guarantees incorruptibility. Incorruptibility helps bring us nearer to God.'"

"What are your laws?" I asked.

"To receive my laws, you must prepare yourself. You must ready yourself for my total embrace. Meditate on me. Ask earnestly for my gifts, and they will be revealed to you. Court my presence as a lover courts the beloved. Enough information has been given to you so that you have knowledge, but you do not yet have Wisdom. So pray, meditate, ask, commit, open and surrender. As you begin to purify your body, your mind, and your heart, I will come to you. And when I fully embrace you, you will know all. And at that time you will not merely teach about me, but you will truly heal by my power."

And with that statement, she released her hand from mine. I felt a tremendous loss. "Please come back," I said.

"I have never left you," she whispered. "And you will never feel separated from me as you court me, seduce me, and merge with my Wisdom."

As she began to dissipate into a lavender-white light, I heard these words, "I will come to you when you are ready, when you are fully prepared. Do not despair. All of your energy systems are opening. Have courage. Have faith. The Archangels and the angels are here for you, to be with you, and to help you with your transformation. You may use this prayer to call me:

"Oh, Shining One. Oh, Angel of Wisdom. Hear my prayer.
Let your powerful healing light envelop
my body, my mind and my soul.
As I radiate with your energy, you are here with me,
my beloved, revealing to me all I need to know.
Oh, Shining One. Oh, Angel of Wisdom. Hear my prayer.
As I touch and pray for others in your name,
my Sophia, healing and wholeness takes place.
You harmonize my soul and I vibrate in perfect peace,
the peace that passes all understanding.
Oh, Shining One. Oh, Angel of Wisdom. Hear my prayer.
You are my love forever, my Sophia,
May your Essence of Wisdom be my Wisdom now."

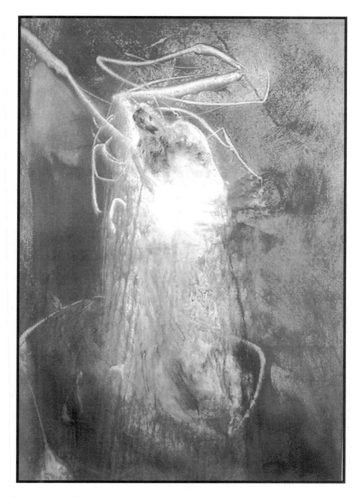

Chapter Fifteen

Metatron – The Archangel of Spiritual Awareness

"I am Metatron, The Archangel of Light. I am the white light of Truth, the Light of all lights. Come forward. Walk into the Light, the Light that you cannot see but that your soul knows. You are now ready for the last step in your journey."

As the lavender-light began to dissipate, I fell to my knees, totally overwhelmed and stunned by this experience and by the presence and power of this Archangel. It seemed that a great amount of time passed. I felt I could never rise again. In this great awe and wonder, I was totally humbled, and then I heard a voice, a voice so deep it felt like an echo in a large cavern.

"Rise and stand on your feet," it said. "I am the first and the last, the Alpha and the Omega."

And as I stood up before the altar, the seventh candle spontaneously lit. Behind the altar there arose a giant white curtain. And the same voice behind the curtain spoke to me, "I am Metatron, The Archangel of Light. I am the white Light of Truth, the Light of all lights. I am the power of spiritual awareness. I stand for freedom, liberation and transformation. I am the Divine Logos and in combination with Sophia, I bring the physical universe, including the Christ into creation. Then God said: 'Let there be light and there was light.' I am the first Light of God. My essence is Light.

"As an Archangel, my power corresponds to the opening at the top of your "psycho-noetic body," called the crown center. When this center is fully open, my energy streams into your body and helps integrate all of the other energy systems, filling them with spiritual power and purpose, illuminating them and allowing you to see your full magnificence as both a human and spiritual being.

"You have asked that the truth about angels be revealed to you, and you have been given knowledge of this truth. Whatever you can understand has been explained to you. Continue to pray. Continue to ask that your energy centers be opened, and you will continue to receive the energy of the Archangels.

'The energy of the Earth will flood your body through the centers of Life, Joy and Power, circulating through your Love center, and reaching out to others. The energy of Heaven shall envelop you as Light, Wisdom and Beauty, circulating into your Love center.

"Heaven and Earth are coming together, masculine and feminine are coming together, mingling, merging, balancing, harmonizing. You are an energy system receiving the energy of God from Heaven and Earth. You are now ready to take this energy and knowledge and return to the Earth. We will always be with you to assist you, to comfort you, to guide you.

"Your guardian angels will help protect you and make your way safe. Know that the entire universe is behind you, supporting you, and that you are never alone."

And then the Archangel said, "Come forward. Walk behind the altar and through the curtain, into the light that you cannot see but that your soul knows. You are now ready for the last step in your journey. Do not be afraid."

And I heard these words, "You may call me to you at anytime with this prayer.

> *"Metatron, Angel of the First Light,*
> *Divine Logos, illuminate my soul.*
> *You are the Light of all life,*
> *Not just the Light that I can see,*
> *But the Light I cannot see,*
> *the Light my soul knows.*
> *Metatron, Angel of the First Light,*
> *Allow me to merge with your Light*
> *and radiate with your Essence.*
> *Pour your Light through me,*
> *bringing together Heaven and Earth in me.*
> *Metatron, Angel of the First Light,*
> *May your Essence of Light be my Light now."*

I stood upright, suddenly feeling a presence and power I had not felt before. I looked at the curtain and walked toward it, and as I did, the white curtain parted. It appeared to me that there was nothing below my feet. I kept hearing the words, "Step forward, move into the light that you cannot see, but the light that your soul knows."

So, on faith, not knowing what was before me, I stepped into the void.

Chapter Sixteen
New Beginnings
"I am born again of the Spirit of God."

ANGEL QUEST

Suddenly, I found myself on the ceiling in a hospital room some-where on the Earth. Looking down below me, I saw a body. It looked exactly like my body sleeping comfortably. Although I wanted to observe the situation from my comfortable vantage point and had no conscious desire to enter this body, I found myself being irresistibly being drawn to it. It was like a magnet pulling me. I just let go and experienced the very conscious sensation of incarnation. It really felt wonderful, like a fantastic sexual experience, but only with myself.

As I slowly opened my eyes, the room came into focus. I heard a familiar voice shout, "He's waking up, he's waking up. Thank, God. He's coming back."

It was the voice of Katherine, one of my meditation partners. The two other people in the room I immediately recognized as Joyce and Scott, close friends from the newspaper.

"Hi," I said. "I didn't mean to scare anyone." My voice felt so strong, I almost scared myself.

"I can't believe it," Joyce said. "One minute totally out, the next minute commanding the room. How are you feeling?"

"Well, I'm a little confused and disoriented," I answered. "Where am I? What happened?"

"Well," Joyce replied, "five days ago, at about 8 p.m. in the evening, you were found by the highway patrol lying face down in a cow pasture, about five miles outside of North Fork. The circum-stances were very mysterious. It appeared that you had driven your car into the field, opened the door, walked about twenty feet, and then laid down on the grass.

"It had been quite foggy that evening, but there were no skid marks on the road, and there wasn't even a scratch on the car. When the police and paramedics arrived, the engine was turned off, the keys were in the car, but the lights were still burning. In fact, that's how you were first spotted. A passing motorist saw the lights and called.

"When they found you, they said you were in a coma, although they couldn't find any overt injuries. At first, they thought you had had a stroke, but all of your neurological signs were normal. You've been in a coma for almost five days, and they couldn't figure out why. After the first three days, the doctors said you might not ever wake up. They just didn't know.

"They first notified Scott of the accident the night it happened, and he told the rest of us."

"You mean you've been here all this time?" I asked.

"Yes," answered Katherine. "The three of us, Joyce, Scott and I, have been coming every day to do a prayer vigil. We hoped we would be here when you woke up."

"It's good to have you back. We've missed you, buddy," said Scott. Scott was grinning from ear to ear, and I couldn't help but grin back.

At that moment, a young man, who looked to be in his early thirties, poked his head in the room. "What's going on?' he asked. "Has our patient returned from the dead?"

The young man, obviously a doctor, strode over to my bedside, pulled out what appeared to be a small flashlight from his pocket, and began peering into my eyes. "I told your friends that you could wake up at anytime, but, frankly, I was skeptical."

"He just woke up, doctor," said Joyce. "Isn't it miraculous! And he looks and sounds great. In fact, if I didn't know better, I'd swear he looks ten years younger, too!"

I smiled and thought, a sign from Sophia. Just a little sign so I'd know beyond any doubt that what I had experienced wasn't a dream.

"I want to get up and weigh myself," I announced, and began to throw the blankets off of me, realizing too late that I was completely naked.

"You can't get up! You have to go about this slowly," Joyce protested, as she rushed towards me, placing her hands on my shoulders and gently pushing me back into bed.

But in that short moment both of us had a quick look at my body, especially my stomach. "My God," Joyce said. "Your beer belly is gone. You didn't tell me you'd been dieting."

"I haven't," I said. "It's something else. Isn't there a robe around here?" I asked, looking around.

Just then an older woman, who was apparently a nurse, walked in and said in a very authoritative voice, "All right, everyone, out. Let this man get dressed. He needs a shave and something to eat. The doctor wants to examine him. It won't take long. Everyone out."

After everyone left, she turned and closed the door. In that ten second period, the whole atmosphere of the room changed from carnival excitement and joy to stillness and quiet. She handed me a robe and turned her back. As I slipped on the robe, I noticed my body was thin and felt very alive. I literally jumped up so I could see in the bathroom mirror. Although I needed a shower and shave, my face appeared young, strong and handsome. I had never looked this good before. Gone were the wrinkles around my eyes and the lines in my forehead. My body felt trim and toned, like I had been working out with a professional trainer.

"Been on an interesting trip?" I heard the old nurse say. That voice. I'd heard that voice before. "If you want my advice," she continued, "I wouldn't discuss this with anyone. They won't understand, and some people might even take offense."

"Cleo?" I asked. "Is that you?" She turned and smiled that same warm, compassionate smile that I remembered. It was a smile that told me that I was deeply loved and that there was really nothing to worry about.

"Well, I thought I'd come by and see how you are doing," she said. "My, my. You do look good. The angels must have treated you just fine. But you know, these people around here won't believe you."

"But I thought I was supposed to be a messenger," I said. "How can I bring information to the Earth if I can't say anything?"

"The time isn't right," she answered. You have all the information, and you won't forget it. It's stored in your memory. You get to remember it all. But right now you need to prepare yourself. You need to continue your meditation practice and learn to meditate with your energy centers.

"But, it is important that at this time, you keep this knowledge to yourself. You will be given a signal at sometime in the future, and you will be told what to do. The timing must be right. If your information is released too soon it will be ignored or worse. There are others on the planet who have had similar experiences. You will meet them over the next year or so. They will share their experiences with you and this will strengthen your resolve. You will find the perfect right vehicle of expression to tell your story and others will come to help you. You will be amazed at all the events that are about to transpire. Remember, don't try to push. Wait until the time is right. When the time comes, you will know exactly what to do, but not yet."

"What shall I tell my friends and the doctors?" I asked.

"Just tell them that you went to North Fork on a story and you got lost in the fog, that there must have been some kind of accident, and you don't remember anything else till you woke up."

"But what about the fact that the car wasn't scratched, I don't have any bruises, I lost thirty pounds, and look ten years younger?"

"Details," said Cleo, with a sly smile. "Mysterious details. They'll shake their heads a little, trying to figure it out, why you were in a coma, why you suddenly woke up from it, but they'll just chalk it up to spontaneous remission or something like that and go about their business."

"But why was I in a coma?" I asked. "And if there is no time in Heaven, why was I here for five days?"

"Your body was in a coma, but you weren't in it," she said, a little annoyed. "And who said there isn't time in Heaven?"

Just then there was a knock at the door. "Can we come in?" Katherine asked.

"Tell them to wait one more minute," Cleo said.

"Just a few more seconds. I'm just finishing shaving," I yelled.

"The last thing I want to tell you is this: When the time comes, you will meet a person. You have seen her before, but you have never spoken with her. She will give you a sign. She will look at you with total love and compassion, and she will say to you, 'Write the truth about angels.' Only then will you start writing. People will come to your aid to make sure your message gets out."

"Can we come in now?" asked Joyce and Katherine in unison.

"Come on in," I said, looking towards the door. I turned to look back at Cleo, and she was gone. She had simply disappeared.

"I can't believe how good you look," Joyce said.

"I can't believe how good I feel," I said.

"Come on, let's figure out how to get me out of here." There was such a feeling of joy in the room. Scott grabbed my belongings. Joyce and Katherine locked arm in arm with me as we left the room, walked down the hall, and out into the bright sunshine.

As I breathed in the wonderful air, I had a real feeling that I was truly at home here on Earth for the very first time.

"God, I love this life," I thought to myself. "I can't wait to find out what happens next."

I didn't have to wait long. From the very day I left the hospital, things began to happen. First, everything in my life seemed to flow in wonderful harmony. Everything felt crisp and new. I looked forward to each day with enthusiasm and joy. I guess my new attitude was contagious, because my friends kept commenting on how wonderful it was to have me back and how much fun it was to grow and share together.

In our meditation prayer group, I continually had a sense that the angels were holding me in their love. I felt that same loving presence that I experienced in the tunnel of light. When I met new people, I felt a connection at a deeper level. I found that I could feel what others were feeling. I experienced their worries and concerns, but I also felt a communion with people at a deep heart-level.

I didn't discuss my experience with anyone. Although nothing seemed to change outwardly in our society and I could often feel the deep pain and frustration of others, I knew that a profound change had occurred in me. Society was still looking for external solutions to problems and quick-fix approaches to success. But, inside, my world had changed. I saw the deep and abiding Love of God behind the external events. I only wished others could have this same experience.

Then it happened. About two weeks after I was released from the hospital, I saw her. It was the strangest feeling. I saw her in the supermarket. I knew that I had seen that face, those eyes, before.

With all of the courage I could muster, I approached her. Her back was turned and I gently touched her shoulder. She turned around, a little startled.

"Excuse me," I said. "I hope I'm not bothering you. But I know I've seen you before."

I expected her to say, "Oh, sure. I've heard that before." But, instead, she looked at me with incredible soft blue eyes and said, "And where was it that you saw me?"

Before I knew what I was saying, I blurted out, "With the angels during orientation."

Her body went rigid, her jaw dropped, and for almost a full ten seconds neither of us spoke.

"Well," she said. "I guess you and I have a lot to talk about. Tell me the truth about angels. Write the truth, I'll help you."

We agreed to meet at my office at the newspaper later that same night at around 8:00 pm. We sat across from each other at my desk, and began talking non-stop for hours. We told each other about our experiences with the angels. Although our experiences were somewhat different, the message was the same. We were to come together with others and tell the truth about the angels. We talked until early morning. It seemed I had known her all my life.

"Don't worry," she said, as she got up to leave. "I'll be around. In fact, I'll see you tomorrow for lunch. In the meantime, you have a job to do. Start writing."

As she left my office, I felt led to sit in meditation. A deep feeling of joy and peace came into my heart, filling my whole being.

And then the voices came to me, the voice of Cleo, the voice of my guardian angel, the voices of the Archangels. "Write," the voices said. "We will help you remember. Write the truth about angels. Don't concern yourself with the outcome. Just write. The ways and means will be provided for your information to become public. You are fulfilling your mission."

As I began to write, I knew everything was unfolding perfectly. I embraced my mission. I felt the energy, the passion, the power, the love of my whole life.

"I am completing the first part of the plan," I thought. "The time is arriving. All I need to do is get out of the way and let it happen." And it is.

Invocations of the Archangels

Each of the Archangels represent a Divine Essence. As you invoke the Essence of each Archangel you establish that Essence within you. To prepare yourself you may first wish to say the following poem.

I am Life and as Life I do flow.
I am Joy above and below.
I am Power so I can let go.
I am Love. I reap what I sow.
I am Beauty. I watch myself grow.
I am Wisdom. I know that I know.
I am Light. I eternally glow.

Now, relax, and watch yourself breathing until you feel a sense of serenity come over you. As you breathe in, visualize spiritual energy filling your entire being. As you breathe out, release all concerns or worries.

You may chant the prayer of one or more of the Archangels. You may wish to end your session in meditation and then say.

May the energies of Heaven fill my conscious-
ness from above. May the energies of the Earth fill
my consciousness from below. May these energies
mingle and merge within me bringing forth the
Life, the Joy, the Power, the Love, the Beauty, the
Wisdom and the Light that I am. Thank You
God. And So It Is.

Prayers of the Archangels

ANEAL

"Aneal, Angel of the Air, Angel of the Earth, Essence of Life,
breathe your life into me now.
Make your stability and order manifest in my life today.
May your presence and energy of the Earth
fill me with the delight of nature.
May I know my connectedness with the earth,
the seas, the rocks, the trees, the plants, the animals and my
fellow humans.
May your Life permeate my soul.
Aneal, Angel of the Air, Angel of the Earth, Essence of Life,
May you fill my entire being with your life energy
I am open, I am receptive, I radiate with your Life Energy now."

CAMAEL

"Camael, Camael, Angel of Joy, come to me now.
Fill me with your passion and enthusiasm.
Let me feel at the deepest level of my being.
As I merge with your energy, let me become totally alive and
intoxicated with your enthusiasm.
I am alive, I am immersed in livingness.
I am passionately in love with life.
I open myself to the true joy of living.
I am receptive to your healing energy of Joy.
I unite with the energy of Life within me.
My life is ordered in pure Joy.
Camael, Camael, Angel of Joy,
May the essence of your Joy be my Joy now."

MICHAEL

'Michael, Angel of Power, come to me now
    and fill me with your clarity and decisiveness
Let me feel your presence so that I may
    act from a clear space of right action.
Allow me to blend your energies into a harmonious whole
Allow me to focus my quiet power ,
    to act decisively from strength but also from great love,
Give me courage, will and determination.
Let me consciously and creatively direct your power,
    focused in love and goodwill
    with the highest and purest intention possible.
I am open and receptive to your Power now
And I bring together my energies of Life and Joy
    and merge them into your Power.
Michael, Angel of Power,
May your essence of Power be my Power now."

GABRIEL

"Gabriel, Gabriel, Angel of Love,
I call on you to open my heart.
Allow me to experience total kindness and caring.
Make my heart full of joy so that I may comfort and
    nurture others.
Let my love touch others and help with the healing process
    of the world, so that each of us feels a sense of unity and
    wholeness.
I know there is nothing that enough love cannot heal.'
Gabriel, Gabriel, Angel of Love,
I am open , I am receptive, I am ready to give of my Love.
May your essence of Love be my Love now."

URIEL

"Uriel, Uriel, Angel of Beauty,
    may your creative energy flow to me,
    a new energy, an energy greater than my previous
    ability to comprehend or believe.
As I open myself to you, I open myself
    to the creative sound of the Universe.
Your musical energy flows through my soul and I hum inside.
I open to new dimensions in Spirit.
My old ways of thinking are changed and transcended,
    and I see the world as bright, shining and beautiful.
And I hear the Word of God singing,
'Behold I make all things new.'
'Uriel, Uriel, Angel of Beauty,
May your essence of Beauty be my Beauty now.'"

RAPHAEL-SOPHIA

"Oh, Shining One. Oh, Angel of Wisdom. Hear my prayer.
    Let your powerful healing light envelop
        my body, my mind and my soul.
As I radiate with your energy, you are here with me,
    my beloved, revealing to me all I need to know.
Oh, Shining One. Oh, Angel of Wisdom. Hear my prayer.
As I touch and pray for others in your name,
    my Sophia, healing and wholeness takes place.
You harmonize my soul and I vibrate in perfect peace,
    the peace that passes all understanding.
Oh, Shining One. Oh, Angel of Wisdom. Hear my prayer.
You are my love forever, my Sophia,
May your Essence of Wisdom be my Wisdom now."

METATRON

"Metatron, Angel of the First Light,
Divine Logos, illuminate my soul.
You are the Light of all life,
Not just the Light that I can see,
But the Light I cannot see,
        the Light my soul knows.
Metatron, Angel of the First Light,
Allow me to merge with your Light
        and radiate with your Essence.
Pour your Light through me,
        bringing together Heaven and Earth in me.
Metatron, Angel of the First Light,
May your Essence of Light be my Light now."

Glossary

The information revealed in this book cannot be understood and absorbed in one sitting. Therefore, we have included a glossary to help the reader come to a deeper understanding of the truth and wisdom about angels. The primary purpose of this glossary is not to educate the reader on the history of angels, but to help communicate the message of this particular experience.

Aneal:
The first of the seven Archangels, Aneal is the Archangel of Life. He corresponds to the first energy system in the "psycho-noetic" body of humans, also known as the "base chakra." His color is red which symbolizes the red Earth and also blood, the substance of the material body. His Life energy is transmitted upward from the Earth into the individual and so His direction is from below.

Angelology:
Angelology is the historical study of angels. Two wonderful books that go into an in depth and unbiased study of angel origins and history are: Godwin, Malcolm. *Angels: An Endangered Species*. New York: Simon and Schuster, 1990, and Lewis, James R. *Angels A to Z*, Detroit, Visible Ink Press. While it is interesting to read about the philosophical and theological speculations of others concerning angels, most of these historical ideas are speculation only. We must ask for direct experience and discover the "truth about angels" for ourselves and not rely on the hearsay opinions of others. Remember, "When you ask with an open heart to know the truth about angels, your request will be granted."

Angels:
The word angel comes from the Greek word *angelos* and means "messenger." Contrary to historical speculations there are only two kinds of angels that affect humans and the Earth, guardian angels and Archangels. Guardian angels have both individuality and per-

sonality. Unlike humans they have only "psycho-noetic" bodies. Their main function is to provide guidance and protection to humans if humans are open to the possibility.

Archangels:

Archangels are great energy vortexes. They are the primary emanations from God and contain the Seven Primary Essences that make up the Universe. These Essences are Life, Joy, Power, Love, Beauty, Wisdom, and Light. These universal energy vortexes correspond to the seven energy systems contained in the "psycho-noetic" bodies of humans. When these Archangels are contacted by humans they will appear to take form and communicate in a way that can be understood. So, to humans they are real individualizations of God, the first emanations of Divine Spirit. In this particular revelation the names they have been given are, Aneal, Archangel of Life; Camael, Archangel of Joy; Michael, Archangel of Power; Gabriel, Archangel of Love; Uriel, Archangel of Beauty; Raphael-Sophia, Archangel of Wisdom; and Metatron, Archangel of Light.

Blake, William:

Blake, (1757-1827) was an English mystical poet and artist who had direct experience with angels in the form of mystical visions. He knew that ultimately universal harmony would be established, that evil would be redeemed, and that the goodness of God would prevail. He also knew that angels are androgynous, blending together both male and female energies.

Camael:

Camael is the Archangel of Joy and is the second of the seven Archangels. Her universal energy corresponds to the second energy system in humans, also called the sexual chakra. Her color is orange which stands for passion. Her direction is from the East which symbolizes the joy of the morning and the rising sun.

Chakra:

Chakra is a Sanskrit word that means wheel of light. According to Eastern religions all people have seven chakras or wheels of light in their etheric bodies. One of the purposes of communing with the Archangels is to open these chakras so that individuals can receive more universal energy. As all seven centers fully open, the individual becomes transparent and fully manifests as a spiritual being.

Cherubim:

Cherubim are not angels. They are mythological creatures invented by the Assyrians to symbolize the guarding of a very sacred place. A cherub is depicted in Assyrian art as a cross between a ferocious animal and a giant bird. The creature is mentioned in the Bible as a guard to the entrance to the Tree of Life.

Dante, *The Divine Comedy:*

Dante (1265-1321) is important in angel lore because he wrote about what happens to the soul after death. His *Divine Comedy* describes a medieval conception of Hell, the sufferings of the unrepentant soul, "Satan", and the idea of purgatory. He had no direct experiences with angels and much of his writing is based on earlier speculation on angels, the devil and Hell. He could be called the Stephen King of the 13th century.

Dionysius:

Dionysius the Areoagite was a 6th century angelologist who speculated on nine levels of what he called choirs of angels. He was influenced by the *Book of Enoch* and the philosophy of Neoplatonism. There is no evidence that he had any direct experience with angels and may have been influenced by the Gnostic teachings of his day. He helped perpetuate the mythology of the separation of God from creation and the separation of Spirit from matter. It was Dionysus who named the order of angels in Heaven. You can read all about these hierarchies and orders, but they have nothing to do with the way the universe actually works.

Enoch, Book of:

During the second century B.C. at least three books were composed in the name of Enoch discussing angels in detail. The name Enoch refers to the patriarch Enoch in the book of Genesis, and how according to legend he did not die as ordinary men but was carried up to Heaven. Much information in these early books became the foundation for angel lore of the early Christian church. The books, themselves, were never accepted as cannon because of the claim that some angels had sex with earthly women. The Church took the position that angels were too pure to ever engage in sex. The books did influence the way the early church fathers viewed angels and was used to explain how the rebellion in heaven took place, where one-third of the heavenly host were expelled.

Gabriel:

Gabriel is the Archangel of Love and is the fourth of the seven Archangels. Her color is green which symbolizes the healing power of love. Her energy system corresponds to the heart chakra or energy system in the "psycho-noetic" body of humans. She is the Archangel who balances the "Heaven energies" from the higher chakras with the "Earth energies" from the lower chakras. Her direction is from "the within" which is the indication of where we must go if we are to find true love.

Jubilees, Book of:

Jubilees is another apocryphal book, like Enoch, written around 135 B.C. which states that the angels were created by God on the first day. They were called Watchers, who descended to Earth to instruct the children of men on righteousness and brought evil into the world by having sex with women. And according to *Jubilees*, angels ate manna, the nectar of the Gods.

Lucifer:

The word Lucifer means "light bearer." According to tradition Lucifer was the most powerful of all the Archangels, but rebelled against God and was therefore expelled from Heaven. Because of the information contained in the *Book of Enoch* and the *Book of Jubilees*, the fall of Lucifer was used by the early Church to explain how Adam and Eve were tempted and how evil found its way into the "good creation" of God. Lucifer was mistakenly equated with "Satan", who was seen as the adversary of God. Lucifer is actually a symbol of light that has been repressed, and therefore turns in upon itself. Lucifer is not a true angel but represents the unredeemed part of humanity, the shadow side of our nature that must be brought into the true Light of God.

Metatron:

Metatron is the seventh of the Archangels and is the Archangel of Light. His energy corresponds with the crown chakra in the human "psycho-noetic" body, the energy center at the top of the head. His color is white light symbolizing illumination. His direction is from above indicating his energy enters into the body from above. Historically, Metatron is first mentioned in 12th century Jewish mysticism and is the highest of the Archangels in the Jewish Kabbalah.

Michael:

Michael is the third Archangel, the Archangel of Power. He corresponds to the third energy system in the human "psycho-noetic" body also called the solar-plexus chakra. His color is gold which symbolizes abundance and prosperity. His direction is from the north which represents focus, will and determination.

Milton, John, *Paradise Lost:*

In his very famous book, *Paradise Lost,* Milton (1608-1674) took all the ideas of angels that existed up to his time and synthesized them into a complete treatise on cosmic forces in the universe. He mentions "Satan", Uriel, Raphael, and Michael as Archangels. and explains how "Satan" and one third of the angels rebelled against God and how there was a cosmic war in Heaven. His ideas of Heaven, the temptation of Adam and Eve, and the fallen angels were accepted by the church and remain today as the basic Catholic theology concerning angels. Unlike The Divine Comedy, there is more optimism in *Paradise Lost* and Milton even shows some compassion and understanding for the sufferings of the fallen angels.

Psycho-noetic body:

The psycho-noetic body is another name for the combination of the mental and spiritual body in the individual. When humans make their transition from the Earth, they leave behind their physical body and travel onward with their psycho-noetic body. Their psychic body contains all of their memories from their earthly and other lifetimes. If they decide to incarnate again, their psycho-noetic body will create another physical body. Angels have psycho-noetic bodies but do not create physical ones although they may take on the appearance of a physical body for a short time.

Raphael-Sophia:

Raphael is the sixth Archangel, Archangel of the Sun, the Archangel of Healing. Her name is also Sophia, the Archangel of Wisdom. Her essence is Wisdom. She corresponds with the "third-eye" chakra in the body. Her color is majestic purple that symbolizes peace. Peace comes to the one who embraces true Wisdom, who seeks total healing. Her direction is from the west and represents sunset and the fulfillment of the day.

Satan:

Satan is a Hebrew word that means 'accuser'. In early Jewish thought, Satan was seen as the obedient servant of God fulfilling his duties as a adversary against humanity. He was not seen as a source of evil until later Judaism was influenced by the dualistic teachings of Zoroastrianism. Unfortunately the early Christian Fathers accepted the myths of later Jewish literature and portrayed Satan as an adversary to God who seduces humanity to sin. They also equated Satan with Lucifer and expanded on the myths of the 'fallen angels'.

Seraphim:
Seraphim were a type of animal monsters derived from the Babylonians. A seraph was a flying serpent with six wings and four faces. They were not considered angels until Dionysius the Areoagite wrote about them in the 6th century A.D.

Theodicy:
Theodicy is the study of how evil permeates a good world and attempts to solve the following riddle: How can evil exist if God is the Creator of everything, God is good and God created a good world?

Thomas Aquinas:
Aquinas, (1224-1274) was important in the history of angelology because he was recognized as the most influential Church theologian of his age. He explained why the existence of angels was absolutely necessary to God's hierarchy. He further perpetuated the ideas of Dionysius and legitimized the ideas of angels within the Church. His fourteen treatises on the nature of angels is wonderful philosophy and theology but has nothing to do with any direct experience of angels.

Uriel:
Uriel is the fifth Archangel, the Archangel of Beauty. He corresponds to the fifth energy center in the "psycho-noetic" body, also called the throat chakra. His color is electric-blue which symbolizes creativity. His direction is from the south which represents the artistic and the creative. He is the creative sound of the universe, the universal Aum.

Artist of the Angels
Joyce J. Gust

The drawings and the beautiful color prints of the angels are the product of the phenomenal artistic talent of Joyce J. Gust. The author discovered her angels, "born of dreams, feelings and intuitions" in the art gallery of Constance Lindholm in Milwaukee, Wisconsin, in June of 1995.

Author and artist met in November and fell in love with each other's work.

Joyce was visually expressing the very angels that Tom felt so profoundly. Both knew that they had been brought together, not by accident but for the purpose of bringing the light of the angels to the world.

"I am compelled to paint these angels," states Joyce. "It's not a cognitive thing but a vision that comes directly from the unconscious. I feel my work is a reflection of the soul connecting me with my Spiritual Source."

Joyce was raised as a Catholic in Milwaukee. As a child she fell in love with the ritual and ceremony of the church. She is a deeply spiritual women who has continued her spiritual quest and has blended her Western religious training with the ideas of the Baha'i faith, Eastern concepts, and spirituality of indigenous peoples. "I've come to my own realization that God, the main Spirit, whatever you want to call It, is everywhere and within all of us," she states.

Joyce now resides in Winneconne, Wisconsin. She received her baccalaureate degree from Marquette and has completed graduate studies at UW-Oshkosh. Over the past six years her award winning paintings, prints and works on paper have appeared in numerous local, regional, national, and international exhibitions.

You may order one of her beautiful prints or posters by filling out the order form on the next page. all prints are limited editions and all posters are personally autographed.

Books, Products and Seminars
From Angel Wisdom™

1. Angel Posters in color, autographed by Artist Joyce Gust.
   Price $20.00

2. Limited edition color prints of any of the angels from Artist
   Joyce Gust.
   Price $150.00

3. Angel Wisdom Engagement Calendar
   Order a beautiful engagement calendar showing the angels from
   Artist Joyce Gust in full color.
   Price $25.00

4. Lessons from the Angels-The Path of Wisdom. Order this ten-
   lesson series explaining in greater detail the teachings of the
   angels and discover how you can become an "angel to the angels."
   Price $25.00

5. Lessons in Financial Freedom-The Twelve Steps of Financial
   Freedom. Order these lessons and learn specifically how to be
   financially free and independent.
   Price $25.00

Angel Wisdom also conducts in-depth seminars exploring the concepts of the book. The emphasis of these seminars is experiential and
include meditation, chanting, music and visual art. Call or write
Angel Wisdom™ for details.

For all orders please send check or money order to Angel Wisdom™,
1029 N. Jackson, Suite 1401, Milwaukee, Wisconsin, 53202. Or
call and place your order at (414) 272-ANGL (272-2645). Please
add $1.00 postage and handling for each item and Wisconsin resi-
dents add 5.5% sales tax.

The Nature of Being Whole ®

Products from

AGELESS DOMINION PUBLISHING

View from the Mountaintop: A Journey Into Wholeness

A Contemplative, Inspirational Book of Poems

An empowering and magical look at love, loss, relationship and the spiritual connection. Breathtaking illustrations bring concepts of lightheartedness, forgiveness, and detachment to life. Readers cherish it as they do a dear friend.

ISBN 1-881300-01-3 Retail: $11.95

"A gentle, clear vision of who we are and what we may achieve. It will help many realize the connection between wholeness and healing."
—Larry Dossey, M.D.

View from the Mountaintop: A Journey to Self-Renewal

Guided Meditation Tape

The soothing and sincere voice of Lee Ann Fagan Dzelzkalns leads the listener along a relaxing path to self-fulfillment. Angelic piano harmonies enhance the visualizations and their message of love and encouragement throughout.

ISBN 1-881300-00-5 Retail: $10.95

"Rich in powerful affirmations, healing imagery and deeply relaxing music. The demo always sells itself."
—J. Chamberlain, High Wind Books

Affirmations on Wholeness

A Collection of Positive Personal Statements

Thought-provoking and self-affirming statements presented on colorful pieces of paper simply and gently assist in reframing thought patterns and enhancing conscious awareness. Choose from six different styles tailored to the specific needs of women, men, couples, teens, children and athletes. All styles are available in a 30-day packet or a reusable jar of 100. Refills are available for the jars. Great for gifts, stocking stuffers, classrooms, group leaders and sports teams.

Retail: 30-day packet—$4.95 / Jars—$14.95 / Jar Refills—$12.95

"I use the Affirmations on Wholeness in all my support groups. Everyone finds they are totally accurate each week, moving them to their next level. A great tool for transformational work."

—Suzy Prudden, Transformational Healer
& Motivational Speaker

To order, contact:

AGELESS DOMINION PUBLISHING

AGELESS DOMINION PUBLISHING

P.O. Box 11546
Milwaukee, WI 53211
(414)332-6775 • FAX (414)332-6566

Your comments, questions and concerns are always welcome!

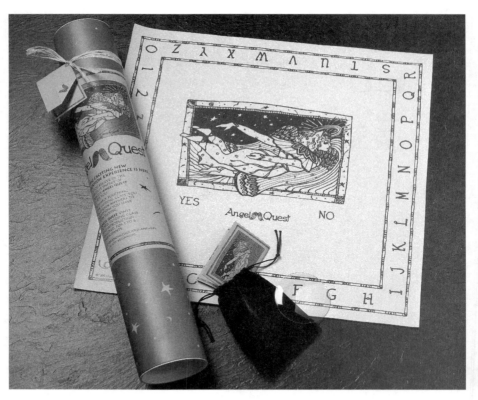

Keep The Company Of Angels

Go on an angel quest!

Angel Quest™, the new communication experience, provides an earthly way for you to summon messages and guidance from your angels. All you need is your positive energy and Angel Quest™.

Angels awaken us to the possibility of exploring questions we may have about our lives. Angel Quest™ encourages your positive thoughts and dreams to come to the forefront, while guiding you to find answers and angelic inspiration. Gather friends and loved ones together to communicate... Afterall, your angels are here for you, so why not summon their help? Angel Quest™ makes a heavenly gift for those who seek a more enlightened life. And the carry-all tube makes it easy to keep the company of angels wherever you go.

$29.95 + $4.50 (Shipping & Handling)
FL Residents Add 6.5% Sales Tax

Check/Money Order   MasterCard   VISA

(Allow 2-3 weeks delivery)

P.O. Box 13063 Tampa, FL 33681-3063 Phone/Fax 813-839-3095 (9-5p.m. EST)